How I Laughed At Depression,
Conquered My Fears And Found Happiness

HIDE
& SEEK

★ Starred Review From *Booklist*

Aron draws on her training as a screenwriter and her experience as a television sitcom writer to tell a hysterically funny account of one woman's quest for happiness. Having battled depression in her twenties, Aron finds that being forced to do the same in her forties is downright, well . . . depressing—even to the point of longing for the good ol' days when psychological problems forced her to be hospitalized. But this time she realizes that she can't rely totally on her beloved therapist but must devise a method to improve herself. Her "master plan" for fixing everything from her relationships with her mother and with men to her weight and health goes awry in multiple ways, all of which she recounts with endearing self-deprecating humor. Among the missteps are a self-help class (in which the instructor preaches that posture is the key to happiness) and a try at speed dating (where one date wept for his dead wife). In the end, Aron finds a "new plan," one that involves acceptance, forgiveness, and gratitude. This engrossing, thoroughly entertaining memoir offers both a delightfully ironic view of the self-help industry and, at the same time, an inspiring personal story of recovery that will resonate with women of all ages and situations.

— Mary Frances Wilkens/*Booklist*

Featured Review From *ForeWord*

There's no lack of self-help books aimed at people who suffer from depression, anxiety, low self-esteem, or neuroses. Nor do we face a dearth of memoirs by people who have been through the excruciating hoops of misery and treatment. So why does the world need Wendy Aron's *Hide & Seek*, which combines her personal story with advice from various professionals she meets during her year of discovery? The answer's simply good medicine: she makes her readers laugh—at the world of self-improvement education, at spiritual gurus, and at ourselves. Learning how to cope with hopelessness has never been so fun.

Aron smartly avoids revealing too much of her emotionally fraught past. After ten years of therapy and a short stint in a mental institution, she knows why she suffers from depression, low self-esteem and a tendency to overeat—growing up in the shadow of a sick sibling with two critical, emotionally distant parents might do the trick for anyone. Now, at 40, she focuses on change. She wants to find a healthy romantic relationship, succeed at her career, and appreciate her friends. To this end, she signs up for a plethora of workshops with titles like "Self-Esteem and the New You" and "Humor and Learned Optimism." Speed dating, a weekend seminar in creativity, and a Weight Watchers membership round out her attempt to create a life of serenity and productivity.

What does she get out of these classes? For one thing, a delicious assortment of one-liners that have a good chance of reducing even the most down-and-out into fits of giggles. But her humor isn't directed solely at the teachers or the other students (she's never cruel)—her funniest moments, and her most touching, come at her own expense. After learning about the "misery gap," the difference between one's real and the ideal selves, Aron observes, "My gap is as wide as the earth's distance from the moon."

Her classes are good for more than just entertainment, however. By the end of the year she realizes she isn't alone in feeling unhappy, that many people are worse off than her. This epiphany carries her a long way toward gaining control over her own perceptions. Aron serves herself up as an inspiration, made easy to swallow with a good laugh.

— Andi Diehn/*ForeWord*

How I Laughed At Depression,
Conquered My Fears And Found Happiness

HIDE
SEEK

A Neurotic's Hilarious Journey
Wendy Aron

KÜNATI

LARGO, USA

HIDE & SEEK

For information, contact Kunati Inc., Book Publishers in both USA and Canada. In USA: 6901 Bryan Dairy Road, Suite 150, Largo, FL 33777 USA In Canada: 75 First Street, Suite 128, Orangeville, ON L9W 5B6 CANADA. Or e-mail to info@kunati.com.

FIRST EDITION

Designed by Kam Wai Yu
Persona Corp. I www.personaco.com

ISBN-13: 978-1-60164-158-8   EAN 9781601641588
Non-Fiction/Body/Mind/Spirit/Self Help/Recovery

Published by Kunati Inc. (USA) and Kunati Inc. (Canada).
Provocative. Bold. Controversial.™

http://www.kunati.com

TM—Kunati and Kunati Trailer are trademarks owned by Kunati Inc. Persona is a trademark owned by Persona Corp. All other trademarks are the property of their respective owners.

Library of Congress Cataloging-in-Publication Data

Aron, Wendy.
  Hide & seek : how I laughed at depression, conquered my fears and found happiness / Wendy Aron. -- 1st ed.
      p. cm.
  Includes bibliographical references and index.
  ISBN 978-1-60164-158-8 (alk. paper)
  1. Aron, Wendy--Mental health. 2. Depressed persons--United States--Biography. 3. Women television writers--United States--Biography. I. Title. II. Title: Hide and seek.
  RC537.W758 2008
  616.85'2700928--dc22
  [B]
                            2008014008

DEDICATION

To everyone who needs help

Contents

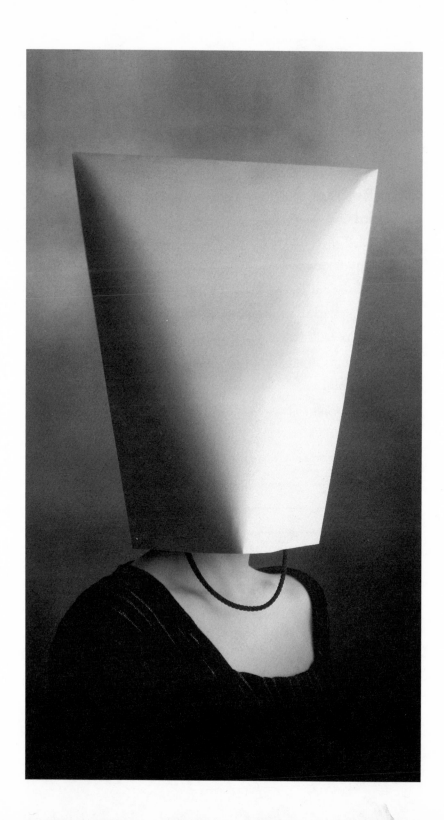

Chapter 1

The Master Plan

Had I been born at the dawn of the twentieth century, I would have been injected with insulin to the point where I would have shaken so violently I'd have fractured my jaw. Then I would have slipped into a coma. If that didn't work, my hands and feet would have been bound and I would have been dunked into a vat of water, or my teeth would have been ripped out.

Fortunately, none of this happened because I was diagnosed with major depression in the latter half of the twentieth century, by which time psychiatric treatments had become as boring as a politician's promises.

However, in spite of my years of relatively benign therapy, when a good friend called to wish me a happy fortieth birthday one evening, I was thinking about a brilliantly conceived suicide.

"What are you going to do tonight to celebrate?" she asked me.

"I'm going to my therapist," I told her, and then mentioned the article I had seen about a man who jumped to his death off the *H* in the *Hollywood* sign. It had once briefly occurred to me to jump off the *Y* when I lived in Los Angeles, I reminded her.

"Well, you're in New York now, so don't think about it," my friend admonished me. "Just blow out the candles at your therapist's."

Although my friend seemed to find it amusing, I didn't think there was anything particularly wrong with seeing my therapist on my birthday. In fact, it was my birthday present to me; I had been treating with Isabel for depression for over ten years, and I considered her to be my closest ally. I had once even asked her why I had to pay her because it was obvious to me that she enjoyed my company as much as I did hers.

Isabel kept tiny purple and gold cards called "Little Miracles" in a bowl next to her couch. They said profound things like, "There's more to life than having everything," and "The best and most beautiful things in the world cannot be seen or even touched. They must be felt with the heart."

Sometimes with seemingly great difficulty, Isabel had successfully steered me clear of the path toward self-destruction that beckons every depressive. With her help, I had avoided having an affair with a married man, quitting a day job that gave me the structure I needed to avoid another depression and letting my father die before making peace with him.

After I got off the phone, I sat on the couch with my cat and took stock of where I was in my fortieth year. I noted that I was facing a half-deaf elderly neighbor whom I wanted to kill for blasting the Home Shopping Network at two in the morning, a job that was in jeopardy because of cutbacks and uncertainty as to whether I would be reassigned, a family that thought of me as "the problem child" and a love life that was on life support. Yes, there were plenty of things to talk to my Hispanic Buddhist social worker about.

When I arrived at Isabel's office at eight, I instantly felt comforted. With its low lighting, bamboo plants, miniature waterfall and scented oil, the place felt like a sanctuary to me. As soon as I settled in on my therapist's couch, I launched into my litany of complaints, ending with the declaration that there were some things about Los Angeles that I missed—like the opportunity to jump off the *Y* in the *Hollywood* sign.

"Los Angeles has nicer winters than here," she said, ignoring my macabre joke. "I might even consider moving there some day."

"And…" I started to say but stopped dead. "What do you mean you're moving to Los Angeles?"

"I didn't say that—"

"You're leaving me?!" I cut her off.

"Perhaps in the future …"

"But what am I going to do without you?" I said, my voice rising.

"It's nothing to think about now," she said. "Anyway, we can always do sessions by telephone."

"But I need to see and smell you," I cried.

"Then I can refer you to another therapist," said Isabel.

"I don't want to see and smell another therapist!" I yelled. "You're my link to reality! What am I going to do?!"

"You're a lot stronger than you used to be," she said. "Don't worry."

"Don't worry?" I exclaimed. "Don't worry. That's like telling a great white shark not to kill!"

After our session I sat in my car for several minutes without turning the ignition on. I was dizzy and my heart palpitated. The only place I felt truly safe was in my therapist's office, and now I was convinced that that was going to be taken away from me. No, wait a minute, I thought. There was one other place and time where I felt secure and at home—it was in a mental institution twenty years earlier.

It had happened like this.

I was in college at Brandeis, a university outside Boston, and decided to spend the second semester of my junior year studying at American University in Washington, DC. Instead of choosing to room in the dorms with another visiting co-ed, I had opted to share a house with a bunch of guys I had met while interning in

Washington the summer before. The reason for this was simple: I wanted my fellow students to marvel at how cool, together and utterly superior I was.

When I got to Washington in the dead of winter, I found that the house I would be sharing was kept at sixty-two degrees. My housemates totally ignored me, and I was on my own for all meals. The day I had to drive to American—about one half hour away from the house—a wicked snowstorm hit, and an Air Florida jet crashed into the Potomac River, effectively cutting me off from the university. It took me three hours to return to the house. I began to panic. The panic spread. I thought I had made a tragic mistake in choosing to go to Washington. I castigated myself for it. I couldn't sleep. I couldn't eat. My housemates ignored me.

I called my parents every morning at six, rehashing all of the mistakes I had made and telling them that I wanted to come home. They told me I would have to go back to Brandeis that semester if I didn't want to stay in Washington. I made panicked calls to Brandeis searching for housing for the winter semester. Once secured, I drove home from Washington having not slept for even an hour in the previous week and turned around and motored up to Boston the next day.

I had lost the apartment that I shared with a friend and was placed in a living situation with roommates who were warring and as inhospitable as the guys in Washington. The one friend of mine who had been an emotional bulwark for me at Brandeis was studying abroad the semester I came back from Washington, leaving me alone with my dark thoughts. Others who knew me said I was "crazy" for coming back from Washington, which served only to compound my feelings of inadequacy. One good friend who was there said, "Wendy, you can't want to feel this way." I didn't know that I had a choice.

My anger about my mistakes turned inward and blossomed

into a deep self-hatred. With almost daily self-condemnation, I worked myself into such a state that I could no longer engage in the simple activities of daily living, like doing my laundry or going food shopping. I was awake 24/7 and somehow forced myself to get to classes, though my mind raced and I couldn't take notes.

In desperation I reached out to a boy on campus whom I had dated when I was a freshman. I was helpless, and he took over, staying by my side day and night. I was consumed by the past, and the only plan I had for the future was to jump in front of a train on tracks that were half a mile from my apartment.

"Do you want to go to a psychiatrist?" my parents threatened me in one of our early morning phone conversations. I didn't answer. My father then insisted I go to the school's counseling center. In the previous few semesters I hadn't even known that such a place existed or where it was on campus. But something in me told me to seek help. When I got there, I told the counselor that I wanted to kill myself.

"Why?" she asked me.

"I have no self-confidence," I mumbled.

"Well, why should you have?" she asked defiantly.

I went and stood beside the train tracks. I wanted to die, but I didn't have the nerve to throw myself on them. I told the boy who was taking care of me, and he called the counseling center. My counselor called my parents and they came up and took me home.

The next day they drove me to an unfamiliar place where a dapper-looking man told us that I would have to be hospitalized. I was so naïve at the time I wondered how wearing a white gown and giving urine samples could possibly solve my problems. I soon found out that in this type of hospital I would not be wearing a white gown, and that the doors would be locked from the outside.

The thing was, though, that after a brief period of indoctrination,

I actually began to enjoy my time in the loony bin. There were the one-on-one basketball games with Eric, a redheaded kid who believed the characters from *Planet of the Apes* were talking to him. There was art therapy, where I was able to make lovely leather change purses that I presented to my horrified mother. And mostly, there was a wonderful stranger with a great sense of humor who was completely sympathetic to my plight. (You can call him my psychiatrist.)

In one session Dr. Trieste drew an analogy between people and tires. Just like tires become worn down through the tread from years of physical abuse, he told me, people become depressed by being worn down from emotional abuse.

"Do you throw out the tire, then?" I anxiously asked.

"No," said my psychiatrist. "We do a patch job."

I stayed with Dr. Trieste for a year following my release from the hospital, during which time I finally got to express all the anger I felt as a child when an older brother who suffered from colitis took all of my mother's attention away from me. As a child, I consistently got the message from my parents that I should not express this anger, and little by little, I had become so disconnected from all of my emotions that I couldn't even identify them. My whole family seemed to suffer from this sickness—arguments went unresolved and feelings were swept under the rug until one day an explosion occurred like the one that sent me to the hospital.

With Dr. Trieste I learned that my posturing as a self-confident, tough, even arrogant individual had been little more than a massive lie. Like most depressives, I had hidden behind this facade to mask profound feelings of inferiority, convinced that if I let people know my true feelings, they, like my parents, would object and not like me. Dr. Trieste taught me that most likely the exact opposite was true, and it was a lesson I took with me to Los Angeles, where I moved to study screenwriting after I graduated from a college in New York.

I ultimately fell out of therapy in LA, and because of it suffered another depression, albeit less intense. I returned to New York to get treatment from a highly regarded new psychiatrist, Dr. Parise, as Dr. Trieste had heartbreakingly moved his practice out of town. Dr. Parise referred me to Isabel, who had become my life preserver. The thought of her leaving me was terrifying. I didn't know how I could possibly face life's difficulties without her. What was I to do?

At our next session I told Isabel that I was reminiscing about my hospitalization and my experience with Dr. Trieste.

"What were you thinking?" she inquired.

"How nice it was. How I was pampered and protected and understood."

"You needed that then," said Isabel.

"I don't think you understand," I said impatiently. "I want to go back there." All I was thinking was: I want to be taken care of.

"You don't belong there now," Isabel told me. "You're coping now."

"No, I'm not," I insisted. "I'm forty years old and what do I have?"

Isabel pursed her lips. "So, you're not happy," she finally said.

"You got that right, sister," I said. And I thought: Not only am I not happy, I am convinced that everyone else is happy most of the time and there is something terribly wrong with me because I don't feel the same way.

"Happiness doesn't come from external things," Isabel said.

"Your Buddhism is very trying on my nerves," I replied.

I know I'm trying on *your* nerves, I thought. We depressives always reject the advice we're given, even if it comes from a trusted professional.

My therapist just stared at me. Clearly she was preparing for another struggle with me. I braced myself for her onslaught, but I had already made up my mind. I wanted those idyllic days with a Dr. Trieste–like figure back. It was then and there that I decided I would find a psychiatrist to commit me. Since Dr. Parise, who now monitored my medication, was not a good sport about this sort of thing, I decided on Dr. Plotnik, the shrink who covered for Parise when he was on vacation. I remembered that Dr. Plotnik had gladly prescribed medication for me at the mere mention of a symptom, so I didn't think he would have a problem with putting me away.

"I was just wondering," I said to Dr. Parise at my next appointment. "What factors do you consider when deciding whether to hospitalize someone?"

"Why do you want to know?" he asked me.

"Just interested," I said casually.

I'm scared. You seem to always be able to read my mind.

"Well," said Parise, "I would see if *someone* was suffering a great deal, if she wasn't functioning or was a danger to herself or others. I'd look to see if that someone had a support system or if she was so disabled that she couldn't meet her own needs. I'd also want to see if she was so involved with drugs or alcohol that I would need to regulate what she could get her hands on."

"Thanks," I said, using all of my strength not to confess my plot to him.

The next day I called Dr. Plotnik's office to make an appointment.

"Who were you referred by?" his receptionist asked.

"Dr. Parise," I said. "He's decided to become a freedom fighter in Mozambique and won't be practicing anymore."

"Oh, really?" she said. "I didn't know that."

After I got off the phone with her, I began to plan my performance in front of Dr. Plotnik. I decided that I would put on a dirty down jacket that I had neglected to get dry-cleaned. I would wear my left shoe on my right foot and vice versa. I would come with a hypodermic needle stuck in my arm. I would tell him that I was an only child and that my parents were deceased. I would threaten to kill myself by taking an overdose of Lomotil. And I would promise to drive my car into my office and take half the other employees with me.

I was brimming with anticipation a few days before my scheduled appointment with Dr. Plotnik.

"Why do you seem so happy?" one of my co-workers asked me. He was so used to the grim expression on my face, he was nonplussed.

"Oh, no reason," I trilled.

The night before I was scheduled to see Dr. Plotnik, I got a message on my answering machine. The voice on the other end sounded like it was in deep distress. "Hello, this is Denise, from Dr. Plotnik's office. Dr. Plotnik has ... Dr. Plotnik has choked to death on a chicken bone and won't be able to see you tomorrow. Thank you for your understanding."

I was devastated. How nervy of Dr. Plotnik to do this to me! Furious, I went to Isabel a week later.

"What's wrong?" she asked me. "You look agitated."

Unable to keep anything from Isabel, I suddenly told her about the whole scheme.

"Why do you think you came up with such a plan?" Isabel asked me evenly.

"Isn't it obvious?" I said. "I want help. If I can get my life into shape, I can be happy."

My therapist's lips curled into a tepid smile, but she said nothing.

"Look," I said. "You're leaving in a year ..."

Isabel held up her hand to slow me down.

"Okay, so there's a chance you might leave in a year," I said, "so I have exactly one year to get my life in order with your help and the assistance of whomever else I can find."

"You've already made great progress," my therapist said.

Not nearly enough, I thought. I believed that somewhere out there, there was a magical solution to my problems that could put me in a state that I heard a psychologist once call "invulnerable euphoria." I knew that it was time to start looking for it.

Chapter 2

Excuse Me for Living

I sat across the desk from a young, tall ice princess whose penetrating blue eyes bored into me like the laser that almost killed James Bond in *Goldfinger*. "Can you name an organizational challenge that you had and how you overcame it?" she asked me.

"What?" I said, having no clue what she was talking about or how it had any bearing on the copywriting job I was applying for within my company. Finally, I hit upon some semblance of an answer, but it was quite apparent that it was unsatisfactory to the human resources drone before me. The woman proceeded to interrogate me for half an hour. Before it was all over I had admitted that some editors I'd worked with were slightly moronic, that I couldn't stand working for high-strung individuals and that there had been some friction between me and the art director with whom I had previously worked.

"Why do you think you said all of those things?" Isabel asked in our next session.

"If I knew I wouldn't be sitting here," I said tartly.

"Do you think it might have been a form of self-sabotage?" Isabel persisted.

"You think it's that again?" I mumbled, with a sinking feeling in my stomach. It wasn't the first time I had heard this phrase in connection with my behavior.

"Well, in a way you rejected her before she could reject you," Isabel said. "It's a dysfunctional form of self-protection."

So there it was. Over ten years after my last depression, my illness still permeated all aspects of my life. It was amazing to me how a simple thing like not being permitted to express my feelings as a child could lead to such bizarre behavior thirty-five years after the fact. But my upbringing, apparently, was going to follow me to the end of my days.

A week later the vice president of creative operations called me into her office. Anxiety and depression are first cousins and I was so nervous about potentially peeing in my pants during our meeting that I made sure to empty my bladder beforehand. When I got there, Tanya, or the Big T, as she was called, clasped her hands on her desk and leaned toward me. "Now, when you say at an interview, 'I've worked for some slightly moronic editors,' how do you think that makes you look?" she asked me.

"Not very good?" I cheerfully ventured.

"It looks like it's not going to work out with that particular book club," she replied somberly. "We'll have to try and find another place for you once your club shuts down, but I can't make any promises."

That night I suffered from the stress-induced insomnia that is so very common to depressives. Some of us have trouble falling asleep, and others, staying asleep. For me, it was waking up at four in the morning in a hyper-alert state, worrying about what the day would bring. The next afternoon, I called Dr. Parise and pleaded for sleeping pills. He must have noted the desperation in my voice, because he acquiesced. He also increased the dosages of my anti-depressant and anti-anxiety medications.

Then I began wondering how non-neurotics stayed so cool under job-related pressure. They didn't sweat or almost pee on themselves like I did. I decided that there must be somewhere to turn for training in how to conduct myself in a professional manner. I looked at a continuing education bulletin that one day landed in my mailbox, and I saw a self-help class that was supposed to show me how to present myself in a way that would get the desired response from others in both social and business situations.

Two weeks later, I lit out for Winning Ways.

When I got to the class, Barbara, our instructor, stood at the front of the room. The former director of a modeling school, she appeared to be in her late sixties and a woman who went to considerable lengths to resist the consequences of aging. Her body was hard and lean from working out, and she wore a generous supply of makeup.

I have nothing in common with this woman, I thought. She is not going to be simpatico. She is like all the teachers I had in elementary school who asked my mother if there was something wrong with me because I looked so sad.

"I'm so glad that this is a small group," Barbara said, surveying the room. "It gives me a chance to personalize the lessons."

Barbara must have realized that we felt this was not exactly good news, because she immediately added, "but not in a way that will embarrass you." Then she pulled a small mirror from her stylish black bag and held it up to her face, moving her bangs back and forth until she was satisfied. I made a mental note to rid myself of bangs before I reached Barbara's age.

Barbara announced that the subject of the first lesson was going to be body language. Then, our intrepid leader walked across the room with her shoulders slouched and her feet scraping against the floor.

That's how I walk, I thought.

"This is how you are never to walk," said Barbara. "It tells people that you hope they'll help you, but that you know they won't."

So this is what I've been telling people all these years. No wonder I can never find an usher to show me to my seat at concerts.

"Now, I can tell that you are in some sort of fashion related business," Barbara said to a woman sitting directly in front of her.

"I'm an interior decorator," the woman said.

"I knew it. The way you accessorize definitely tells me that you bother."

For the first time I looked carefully at the woman. She was very thin and dressed in tight-fitting jeans, with a blouse, belt, shoes and handbag that were all the same shade of pastel blue. I looked down at my own attire, which included a cotton turtleneck with sleeves that were so stretched out they covered my palms.

"You didn't sit in a corner," said Barbara to the woman, casting an eye in my direction. "Your body language takes charge. You say, This is my area. This is my space. This is who I am."

I'm always stepping away from my space to give it to other people, I thought.

At this moment a woman dressed in brown entered the classroom and sat next to the blue lady. "You," said our instructor, as though she had discovered the Holy Grail. "The color tones you picked are superb. You didn't pick black. You chose brown. And do you know why? No. You just know."

"Yes," said the woman hesitantly.

Flashback: I'm shopping with my mother at Macy's and I pick out an olive green sweater and triumphantly bring it back to the dressing room. "How could you pick such a color?" screeches my mother. "Your complexion looks terrible with green!" I slink back to the showroom and stuff the sweater away on the nearest shelf.

Back to class: At this point, Barbara pulled out some handouts and passed them around. I looked down at the sheet, which was entitled, "The 7 Points of Good Body Alignment."

"The first point is that your weight is centered on your feet," said

Barbara. "It's as though there is a tube down the center of your body. You're not falling forward. You're affirming, This is my space."

I wondered what it would actually feel like to have a tube going down the center of my body, short of an endoscopy, but Barbara was on to the next point, which had to do with knee position.

"You have to flex your knees," she said, "but you have to angle your feet in such a way that you don't break your neck."

What do you do if you do break your neck while your knees are flexed? I wanted to ask, but decided against it.

Flashback: I'm ten years old and sitting at the dinner table with my parents and sickly older brother. I make a joke that my brother has no friends. My father gives me a withering look and shakes his head "no."

Back to class: Our teacher won't think my little joke is funny or even germane, I thought. Your sense of humor is perpetually unappreciated.

Now Barbara was on to the next point, which was to pull your stomach in. "Give yourself the gift of life," said Barbara. "I don't want that passive, 'I'll make the best of it' posture."

I looked down at my stomach with the realization that it was always protruding in some fashion, and that I was always trying to make the best of it. What do I do? How do I get out of this class unobtrusively? *Help me!*

Barbara proceeded to skip over points 4, 5, 6 and 7 and got right down to business with a notation to us that all bags and briefcases were to be carried to one side of the body, not clutched in front. "You are telling people that you are spiritually and intellectually equal when your handbag is to the side," said Barbara emphatically.

From the discussion of proper handbag presentation, Barbara segued into the subject of putting one's coat on and taking it off. "When you take your coat off properly, you are saying that your life is God-given," said Barbara.

While I contemplated whether God really cared about the way I took off my coat and marveled at the confident way in which Barbara delivered her absurd aphorisms, our leader announced that she wanted to go around the room and get to know us a little better. "I'm sensing a little bit of shyness in you," said Barbara to a woman sitting at the first desk next to the wall. The woman wore an ill-fitting raincoat and appeared to be wilting.

"Well, I am shy," said the woman. "I'm a mother and a wife and I haven't been out much. I'm really just getting back into life."

A wife and a mother, I thought. Wow. I haven't even accomplished that.

"How tall are you?" Barbara pointedly asked the wilting woman.

"Five foot seven," said the woman.

"You have a nice long stem and you can capitalize on that," said Barbara. "You have a physiology you can do something with."

As compared to me, I thought. Barbara appeared to glance at me. What was she thinking? That I had a short, ugly stem that I couldn't capitalize on?

"Thanks," whispered the woman.

Then Barbara was on to the blue lady, whom Barbara had complimented on her accessories. "Why did you take this class?" asked our instructor.

"I'm in the midst of a painful divorce that involves another woman," said the blue lady, "and—"

Barbara apparently saw this as a golden opportunity to vent and interrupted the blue lady to tell us that she had been a widow for ten years and had a group of other older single women she socialized with. "I know this couple and they hate each other," said Barbara. "I've had 'discussions' with the man, but his wife is one of my dear friends."

None of us knew what to make of this, but Barbara was undeterred. "I had issues with my husband," she said. "My husband was just like my mother. As long as everything looked good on the outside, it didn't matter how you felt inside."

The class did its best to look sympathetic, but it wasn't our sympathy that Barbara was after. It was our respect. "You shouldn't give anyone permission to give you validity. You're given the right to live. Don't let anyone take that away from you," she said, fixing her lapel.

Clearly, you are a woman who knows how to take care of yourself, unlike me, I thought.

After a few more minutes on her r-e-s-p-e-c-t jag, Barbara moved to a Hispanic woman seated to her left.

"I've had health issues," said the woman. "I lost my eyesight, my job and my driving ability."

If I had lost all that, I would have killed myself, I thought.

"Ohh," said Barbara.

"I had Graves disease."

"Ohh," said Barbara again. "I know about health problems. I had a cataract operation, and the doctor left a stitch in my eye, and he was treating it as an infection, but then I met this wonderful doctor. His name was Dr. Ying."

"Dr. Ying?" said the Graves woman hopefully.

"Yes, he's right out here and he cares. I can give you his number."

"I think I was meant to be in this class today," said the Graves woman. Barbara went on and on for several more minutes about the virtues of Dr. Ying, but when she sensed that we were no longer interested, she moved on to me. "Do you have an advanced degree?" she wanted to know.

"Yes, a master's," I said.

"And what do you do for a living?"

"I'm a writer," I said. Barbara looked slightly taken aback. What was that look on her face? Did she think writing an unworthy profession? Or was it that I looked too stupid to actually be a writer?

"I could tell you were the studious type," Barbara finally said. Then she immediately moved on to the next person, a very stiff looking woman with a bright red coat. "Are you married?" she asked the woman.

"Divorced," said the woman sourly.

Barbara must have thought this was another opportunity to shed some angst because she embarked on a discussion about two dates she had had recently. "One was with a retired judge, and all the women were *yes*ing him to death. The other was a construction worker type and he had a lot of ladies."

The divorced woman looked at Barbara suspiciously. It sounded to me like both men had dumped Barbara, but whereas I would never confess such a thing to a bunch of strangers, she apparently had no qualms about it.

"We're all screws and we have to find the right holes," said Barbara, somewhat flustered by the divorced woman. Then she tried to get back on course. "And what do you do for work?"

"I work with attorneys," the woman said as though she did not want to discuss it further.

"Are you a court reporter?" Barbara persisted.

"No," said the woman bluntly.

"Are you a secretary?"

"No," said the woman.

"So you're a, a ..." said Barbara, finally stymied.

"I'm a supervisor," said the woman.

This is the type of woman that would make mincemeat of me in an office setting, I thought.

"I see that you are very set," said Barbara cautiously. The woman flinched, but said nothing. "Well," said Barbara, trying to move the class along. "Now I want each of you to come to the front of the room and pretend you're talking to me." She pointed to the shy woman against the wall, indicating that she go first. The shy woman got up and shuffled to the front of the class. "Now stand against the wall," barked Barbara. The shy woman did as she was told. "Don't come forward with your hands," said Barbara.

"But ..." said the woman.

"If you do come forward with the hands, then keep the shoulders back," commanded Barbara.

"But ..." said the woman.

"Feel like there's a rod going up your center," said Barbara.

"But ..." said the woman.

"Keep your chin straight," Barbara said.

"I'm kind of uncomforta—"

"There's something in there that is not real," Barbara said, cutting the shy woman off. "Now walk over to the radiator."

The shy woman tentatively moved toward the radiator.

"Don't walk so flat-footed," Barbara said. "I want briskness in your step. Don't apologize to me." The shy woman continued to move as though she were sleepwalking. "Come on, now," snapped Barbara. "I'm not going to let you get away with this."

With what? the woman looked like she wanted to ask.

"There's timidity in your nature," Barbara continued. "Don't give in right here," she said, pointing at the woman's stomach.

After several more minutes of torture, Barbara let the shy woman go back to her desk and motioned for the Graves woman to come to the front of the class. Maybe I'll do better than the shy woman, I thought. As the Graves woman carefully positioned herself against the wall, Barbara said, "You've been through hell and back with your health, but you've been loved and protected and cared for."

"Yes," said the Graves woman.

I wish I were loved and protected and cared for.

"You must have an extra sense," the Graves woman told Barbara.

"That's who I am," said Barbara, positively beaming as she gestured for the woman to walk across the room.

Why do other people take such pride in themselves for such stupid things, whereas I could cure cancer and not give myself credit?

"I want a cultured and refined look," Barbara continued. "Eliminate the swing." The Graves woman tried to do as she was instructed but still appeared as though she was about to break into the Charleston.

After the Graves woman, Barbara put the blue and brown women through their paces as I looked on quite anxiously. Barbara complimented them on their accessories and color choices, which made me extremely alarmed, as I had neither accessories nor evidence of color coordination in my attire.

When it was my turn, I nervously approached the front of the room. Barbara gave me the once-over and seemed to be thinking that she was up to big challenges. "Stand against the wall," she ordered me.

"I have poor posture," I mumbled, but I didn't think Barbara heard, or, if she did hear, she chose to ignore me.

She's thinking that I'm a depressive, but she doesn't want to let me off the hook, I thought. Of course, I was mind reading again, something we depressives do compulsively.

"Keep your chin up," Barbara said as I tried to pretend there was a rod going through my body. "There," she said, positioning my body and standing back to gauge her work. "Now, put your hands behind you casually and walk forward. I tried to do what Barbara told me to, but was extremely uncomfortable. "Keep your chin up,"

Barbara exhorted me. "Suck your stomach in. Keep your shoulders back."

After a few more seconds of awkwardness, I finally felt like I was complying with all of Barbara's orders. The only problem was that I was no longer breathing. I wanted to raise this point with her, but before I knew it she was commanding me to walk over to the radiator. "None of this forgive-me-for-living walk," she shouted after me.

Oh, God, she's got me totally figured out.

"That's the kind of walk my ex-husband is going to have after our divorce," commented the blue lady as I moved. A few seconds later, I was back on Barbara's side of the room and she directed me to sit in the chair next to her. "Move your derriere back on the seat," she instructed me. "Cross your legs. Move them to one side. Clasp your hands."

I did my best to meet Barbara's demands. After a few more seconds, she stood back and surveyed her handiwork. "That's what I'm looking for," she said. "Okay, honey."

Glad to have escaped, I got up and scurried back to my seat. I soon learned, however, that I was not in the clear. Before the class ended we were going to learn how to take off our coats properly. Barbara picked up her jacket and demonstrated a complicated five-step process that I was sure I could never master. It went like this: 1) Drop both shoulders of the coat down your back by grasping the lapels on either side. 2) Reach around in back with both hands and grasp both cuffs in the right hand. 3) Remove the left arm from the sleeve and bring both cuffs to the front of the body on the right. 4) Take both cuffs in the left hand and remove the right arm from the sleeve. 5) Grasp the middle of the collar with the right hand and, keeping hold of both cuffs with the left, place the coat over the outside of the left forearm. By the time it was my turn, I had concocted a lame excuse about the bulkiness of my coat.

"My coat is hard," I mumbled. *I'll never be able to do this.*

"Yes, I know it's difficult, honey," Barbara said.

I made a half-hearted attempt to take my coat off gracefully, but Barbara refused to let me get away with it. "Try it again, honey," she said.

I was hoping that you would just do it for me.

I tried it again with equally disastrous results.

"You have to grab the sleeve and swing it around," she said, losing patience.

"Oh," I said. *I've failed this whole class. I'm a failure.*

"Then you have to grab the collar," Barbara continued.

"Oh!" I said.

Somehow, after struggling for several minutes, I finally managed to withstand Barbara's scrutiny. At the end of the class, Barbara informed us that the next session would be dedicated to fashion and that we should wear apparel that reflected a "positive presentation."

I don't even know what that means!

As I left, I had every intention of not showing up.

"How did you do it?" my friend Marie asked when I explained how I had survived the first class.

"It wasn't like I disarmed a nuclear weapon," I pointed out.

"But, still…" said my friend.

The fact that someone was actually impressed with something I had done was all the impetus I needed to enter the room for the remaining class in a black pants suit and a turquoise turtleneck that I hoped conveyed a "positive presentation." As soon as I crossed the threshold, I was accosted by a woman who looked like she had just lost her cot at the homeless shelter. She was wearing three wool sweaters and an overcoat that looked like Salvation Army issue. Her blonde, curly hair appeared not to have been brushed in days and, in addition to tilting to one side, she had a hump in her back indicating advanced osteoporosis.

"What town are you from?" she asked me.

"Rockville Centre," I said, trying to think if I had ever met her before.

You're in even worse shape than I am.

"I'm from Valley Stream," she said. "Do you think you could drop me off on Hempstead Turnpike after class?"

"I have to be somewhere," I said hurriedly.

"I just need to catch the bus on Hempstead Turnpike," she insisted.

"Okay," I said reluctantly, wondering if she had a knife hidden in one of her sweaters. By this time, the supervisor, the Graves lady, the brown lady and a woman who looked like she could be a model had taken their seats in the classroom. The homeless lady mumbled to herself and then tried to get into a conversation with the Graves lady, who was considering her the way one would approach a pool of vomit.

"It was so hot in my house this morning," said the homeless lady. "It was like eighty degrees."

You mean you actually have a home? I wanted to ask.

"You need to open a window," said the Graves lady plainly and then looked away. The homeless lady did not seem to be insulted by this at all. Nor did she seem conscious of the way the others who had gathered for the class were looking at her out of the corners of their eyes. The homeless lady smiled brightly.

At this point Barbara entered the class carrying a large tote filled with scarves of every conceivable color. "I wonder if all my parts are together," she said, withdrawing her mirror from her handbag and playing with her bangs again.

Why don't I ever fix my hair before going out? Am I a total misfit like the homeless lady?

"Have you been a teacher for long?" asked the homeless lady.

"Yes," said Barbara, sizing up her next big challenge. "I've been doing this for years."

"I was a kindergarten teacher," said the homeless lady.

"Wonderful," said Barbara with the same tone one might use to convey information to a retard or toddler. She looked around the room and smiled warmly at all of us who had had the courage to come to the second class. "I'm glad you all came back," she said.

She's just being nice. She's really not impressed by me.

"Now, today we're going to see if you have an instinct about what looks good on you," said Barbara. "Sometimes you know what looks good on you, but you don't know why. During this class we're going to find out why."

So few things look good on me. And when they do look good on me, my cat destroys them with her claws.

"This is a very scientific process," Barbara said, distributing a handout to us. "Color is one's first consideration and is based on hair, eyes and skin tone. If the color doesn't work, nothing works," Barbara stated.

I'm forty years old. I should know what colors look good on me!

"What color do you think looks good on me?" piped up the homeless lady.

"We'll get to that," said Barbara, launching into a discussion about how one is supposed to dress for the occasion. "I know someone who has nothing but dressy clothes, but she doesn't go anywhere," she said. "She's a stay-at-home mom. Isn't that ridiculous?"

"Oh, that's funny," said the homeless lady.

By this time, Barbara had already tuned her out and was making her last point, which was that "fashion is always taken into consideration, but line and fit always precede your decision. It might be 'in fashion' to wear a lot of nudity, but do you look good with your navel exposed?" Barbara asked rhetorically. "I don't think so."

The homeless lady laughed and looked around to find support, but none was forthcoming. I looked down to see if my navel was exposed but it wasn't. "Now," said Barbara, as though she was in the midst of explaining a complex algebraic equation, "there are three basic colors—black, navy and brown—and one uses another color to complement your basic color."

"Oh, that's a fantastic point," chirped the homeless lady.

What if no colors look good on me? I thought. What if I get up in front of the class and make a total fool of myself again? What if I'm the only one who doesn't have a basic color? What if our leader tells me to go shopping with the homeless lady because I'm as hopeless as she is?

"The information you are about to get isn't often given at this price level," Barbara said.

We all looked very unimpressed, so she went on and pointed to the supervisor to come up and be the first victim.

"You should start with somebody else because I've already done this," stated the supervisor.

She's a match for Barbara. I'm not.

"But, uh … uh," said a very flustered Barbara. Then she hit on an argument to woo the supervisor: "But you can teach the others."

The supervisor reluctantly nodded in agreement and got up out of her seat. As Barbara placed her against the wall to review last week's lesson on posture, the supervisor seemed so rigid it looked as though she would snap in half.

"Do something with your feet and your hands," said Barbara. The supervisor defiantly shifted her weight from one leg to the other.

"Now sit down in the chair flush on your derriere." The woman did as she was told. "I love what you've done with the pants suit and the black boots," said Barbara, trying to make peace. "I love how you've used the same color tone and are giving it direction with your hair."

"Thanks," said the supervisor, still on guard.

"Now pick up the mirror and look at yourself," said Barbara. "This is for you, not me."

Barbara circled the supervisor once, the way a drill sergeant might approach a new recruit, and then started playing with the woman's hair. "If your hair were just a bit shorter," she said tentatively, "it might open up your face and soften your chin line."

The supervisor looked like she was about to raise an objection, but Barbara headed her off by rummaging through the scarves in her tote. First, she picked out a brown scarf. "Now, tell me why brown is a no-no for her," she said to the class.

"Her skin tone?" said the Graves lady.

"Exactly!" enthused Barbara.

Why is she so impressed with the Graves lady? What's so great about the Graves lady?

Clearly the Graves lady was becoming the teacher's pet and I deeply resented it, in much the same way I resented my sickly older brother being my mother's pet.

Barbara next brought black and fuchsia scarves together and held them up to the supervisor's face. "These colors are just dynamite for you," Barbara stated. "Look at that. Isn't it marvelous?" Barbara asked the class. We all nodded in agreement as Barbara held scarf after scarf to the supervisor's face, commenting on the appropriateness of each color. "Yellow, orange, brown. These are colors that should never be on your body," said Barbara at one point.

"I look good in yellow," said the supervisor bluntly.

"No, I don't like yellow on you," said Barbara.

I'm so wimpy, I have no opinions.

The supervisor opened her mouth, but no words came out.

"I like gray," said Barbara, holding another scarf up to the supervisor's face.

"I don't look good in gray unless it's silvery," said the supervisor.

I was in awe of the way the supervisor stood her ground against Barbara. That's something you should do, I thought.

"Yes, silvery. Definitely silvery," said Barbara, at last caving in.

After a few more disagreements, Barbara dismissed the supervisor and motioned for the homeless lady to come forward. As she took full measure of her for the first time, Barbara glanced at her watch to indicate that there simply weren't enough hours in the day to get this particular job done. "Everybody who has special needs should stay after class," Barbara finally announced, "so we can address them on a personal basis."

"Does that include me?" asked the homeless lady.

Barbara's also talking to me, I thought.

"Yes, dear," said Barbara, placing the homeless lady against the wall to analyze her posture. Finally, Barbara simply said, "There's a lot of stuff going on."

"Yes?" said the homeless lady hopefully.

"Take your sweater off," Barbara suggested. The homeless lady took off her beige wool cardigan to reveal a lavender sweater hanging limply on her body. Barbara walked over to her and tried to adjust her torso. "You're tilted," Barbara said, clearly frustrated.

"I carry a lot of heavy things," said the homeless lady.

"Yes, dear. But what you're saying is, 'Please accept me.' I want you to take command. People must understand that they are not in a better position than you."

"Okay," said the homeless lady. Barbara instructed her to walk across the room, at which point my fellow student moved in a style reminiscent of the bride of Frankenstein. Barbara shouted directions after her as the rest of us looked on in horror. After what seemed to me like an embarrassing eternity, Barbara let the homeless lady sit down in the chair. I looked at her and noted that she was completely unfazed.

"I love the lavender sweater," Barbara said with considerable effort. "It brings the blue-green out in your eyes."

"Thank you," said the homeless lady, looking completely self-satisfied.

Barbara's never complimented me.

Now our instructor sifted through her scarves. "I think your basic color is navy," she said to the homeless lady. "You should stay away from black and brown."

"Oh, really? I didn't know that," said the homeless lady. Barbara tried to look at her sympathetically, but all she could apparently muster was the appearance of deep pity. After a few more moments that I would have considered excruciating, she let the homeless lady return to her seat. At this juncture, I was convinced that I could not fail as badly as my predecessor, but at the same time I glanced over at her, and she looked like the cat that ate the canary.

"Next," said Barbara, pointing at me. As I made my way to the front of the room I could feel her assessing me. "Weren't you wearing a coat on the way in?" she asked.

Suddenly, I was terror-stricken. I had again worn my bulky, unflattering winter coat, and Barbara, with her eagle eye, had caught sight of it.

"Ye … yes." I managed. "But … I meant to wear a black blazer. I just didn't realize it was this warm out."

You should have known what coat to wear.

"I'd like to see you all in black," said Barbara.

"I have a black jacket," the supervisor said.

I walked over and retrieved the jacket, put it on and stood against the wall, positively petrified about what would come next.

"Bravissima!" said Barbara, applauding me. "That looks great."

The rest of the class nodded in agreement. I was filled with dread.

Flashback: I win a poetry-writing contest in high school and get flown to Albany to meet the governor of New York. The other winners are laughing and smiling at the reception. I sit there, morose. I am convinced that this is just a stroke of good fortune and will surely be followed by some type of horrible retribution. I can't be too happy. I'm waiting for someone to accuse me of something like plagiarism, or worse.

Back to Winning Ways: I thought I was going to be released, but Barbara now ordered me to walk across the room. As I started out, I could hear and feel my heels scraping against the floor.

"I want you to flex your knees and land on the balls of your feet," Barbara barked after me.

I tried to do as she instructed, but I suddenly realized that I might also look like the bride of Frankenstein. By the time I took my seat in front of the class, I was totally flummoxed.

"Now, take the mirror," Barbara said. "Remember, this is for your benefit."

I looked in the mirror and saw what appeared to be a chipmunk storing nuts for the winter.

Barbara started her scarf routine with me, ultimately deciding that I looked best in colorful prints. "I'd like to see you in earrings and a diminutive chain," she advised me as I took my seat in the back of the room.

"I know. My mother is always yelling at me to get my ears pierced," I reported.

"But you don't like to bother," said Barbara, leveling at me what I believed to be her most severe charge.

I'm such a putz, I thought. As the class continued, I could barely pay attention to the casualties in the front of the room. I wondered if the homeless lady had singled me out for a ride off the campus because she had seen in me a kindred spirit, and if Barbara lumped me in the same category as well. I'm such a putz. I'm such a putz.

After a while, I became aware that the class was continuing. Barbara took out a cassette player and told us that she was going to use "this mean machine" to help us learn how to speak properly. She readied a cassette tape and with a great flourish withdrew a sheet of paper from her tote bag.

"We're going to read a poem called 'The Highwayman,'" she said, and dramatically read the beginning of the verse. "The wind was a torrent of darkness amongst the gusty trees," she intoned. "The road was a river of moonlight over the purple moor..." After she finished reading the verse she popped the tape into the recorder and motioned for the homeless lady to come take a seat at the front of the class.

"Read the poem to yourself first," said Barbara. "And when I say 'start,' begin speaking."

The homeless lady looked over the poem. I noticed that she was wearing a grotesque amount of pink and lavender eye makeup and a necklace of pink beads that appeared to come from a 99-cent store. But she did not seem self-conscious in the least. Barbara signaled her to commence with the poem, and as she did so, our instructor took copious notes.

"Did you hear what I heard?" said Barbara after the homeless lady had finished reading the poem. We all looked at her in a non-committal way, clearly uncomfortable picking on someone with such glaring inadequacies. "It was too fast and it was on one level," said

Barbara. "It never moved around."

The homeless lady smiled at Barbara as though she believed she was talking to a third party.

"When I first met you, I got the feeling that you were running away with yourself," Barbara continued. "You were very jittery and too fast."

Suddenly it seemed to dawn on the homeless lady that she was being criticized. "Well, I was a kindergarten teacher, so I was constantly on the run," she said in her own defense.

Clearly, the homeless lady was not a depressive, because she did not blame herself or anyone else for her deficiencies.

"Yes, dear," Barbara continued, "but it doesn't create a sense that you're intact." Barbara then made a series of suggestions that could hardly be called diplomatic.

If she makes these suggestions to me, I'll crumble, I thought.

At the end of the horror show, Barbara motioned for me to take a seat in front of the class. I was relieved, in the way that a comedian is when she follows an act that has bombed. I grimaced as Barbara handed me the poem and turned the tape recorder on. She pointed at me to start talking and I began to read. As I went through the verse, I could feel my voice quivering.

"Now," said Barbara, when I was done, "I get the impression that you're uncomfortable with verbalization."

"Oh?" I said worriedly.

"You're not using your speech to communicate," she said.

Then what am I using it for—to stick a plum up my ass? I wanted to say. I realized that this was childhood anger manifested as adult hostility.

"I know a lot of times we feel self-conscious," Barbara went on. "But we can't present ourselves that way."

"Oh?" I said, smarting.

"What do you do for a living?"

"I'm an advertising copywriter," I said.

"So you don't work with people," said Barbara, and I contemplated what my co-workers would think of this judgment.

"Yes, I work with words," I said meekly.

"And are you single or married?"

"I'm single," I whispered.

Apparently this was all the permission Barbara needed to go off on me. "I'd like to see some color next to your face," she said. Then she walked over to the supervisor and borrowed her red, black and white print scarf and draped it around my neck. "You see?" Barbara said, taking out her mirror and holding it in front of my face.

I still don't look so great.

I nodded glumly as Barbara nearly strangled me ripping the scarf off my neck.

"I'd like to see brown and beige eye makeup," Barbara said. "And I'd like to see some highlights in your hair, so it doesn't blend with your skin."

At this point, I felt too defeated to even comment on the fact that I did have highlights, but that they had almost grown out and I was going to get a new treatment at my next beauty parlor appointment.

"All you're doing is this," said Barbara, lifting her hands up, palms out, to hide her face and push people away. "You have to learn to package yourself."

"Huh, uh," I mumbled, completely crestfallen.

"I don't want to be religious, but God gives us just one shot," Barbara concluded.

I schlepped to the back of the room and slumped into my chair. I was totally defeated.

"Can you walk a little slower?" the homeless lady pleaded as she hobbled after me to my car after class.

"No," I said.

"I bought these shoes for seventeen dollars and they hurt my feet," the homeless lady babbled. "And then when I tried to return them, they wouldn't let me because I didn't have the receipt, and then they told me that I could exchange them and …"

"Look," I said, "there's a bus stop right on campus." I pointed to an area where a bunch of students waited.

"Hey, you guys!" yelled the homeless lady. "Does this bus go to Hempstead?"

I didn't wait to hear their response. I just kept walking to my car. When I got there, I realized the homeless lady was no longer in sight. "I am not like her," I repeated to myself twice. Then I got into my car and sped away.

The following morning, I put on an ample amount of blush and eye makeup and got dressed for work in a black pants outfit and a red cashmere sweater. When I got to the office, I tried to walk to my supervisor's office on my toes. As I sat down on a chair there, I crossed my legs at the ankles, pushed my derriere to the back of the chair and clasped my hands in my lap. I noticed dark circles under my supervisor's eyes, courtesy of another night with her infant son.

"I have a question about an assignment," I said slowly in a modulated voice. My supervisor put her pen down and looked at me. This was probably because I never asked her questions about my assignments. I typically would just nod my head and whisper "okay" when given a task and then worry about what was required afterward. "I need to know if I can write about my experiences as a playwright on the New Horizon's lift note."

"Of course you can," she said.

"Thanks," I said.

"Don't hesitate to ask if you have any more questions," she offered.

"I won't," I said.

It wasn't much, but it was a start.

Chapter 3

Confessions of a Victim

Try as I might, I could only remember my low points in Winning Ways. Absolutely nothing had gone right, I thought. It was a total fiasco. I am a complete loser. Then it occurred to me that sinister forces were on the loose in my psyche. Of course I knew that behind every good depressive lurks a human being with poor self-esteem. In fact, my mother would constantly tell me things like, "I don't know where you get this low self-esteem from," as though she had absolutely nothing to do with it.

Flashback: I'm ten years old. My mother is sitting at the kitchen table and asks me to bring her a cup of coffee. Before I embark from the counter with coffee in hand, she says, "Are you sure you can do this? Are you really certain you can do this? I'm afraid you can't do this. You're going to spill the coffee."

I take a few very tentative steps forward with the coffee, but I am shaking because I'm so afraid that I am going to drop it.

Enter my father. Now I am so nervous I drop the coffee.

My father says, "Oh, Jeez, you dropped the coffee. How could this happen? How could you do that? What is wrong with you? Let me bring the coffee from now on!"

My mother cleans up the spill. I never learn that I can bring the coffee without spilling it. I never learn that I can do much of anything.

Back to the present: My mother said, "Why don't you take a class in self-esteem building?"

Why don't you take a class in building the self-esteem of a child? I wanted to say, but I didn't waste my breath. My mother believed that lack of self-esteem was some humiliating defect you were born with, like a third arm. Consequently, I was so ashamed of my low self-esteem that I couldn't even admit to it to anyone but Isabel. Yet I knew that if I did not address the problem, I would never be able to hold my own in the world. How could one go through life basing her own self-estimation on what others thought of her without suffering from severe mood swings? That's when I decided to sign up for a class called "Self-Esteem and the New You."

When I arrived at the classroom on the appointed day, it was filled with women from a wide spectrum of ages who all smiled at me warmly. Yes, I'm also a member of the I'm-a-bug-under-a-rock club, I thought, taking my usual seat at the back of the room.

A few minutes passed and then a man who looked like an ex-Marine entered the classroom and asked us what we were doing there.

"We're here for the self-esteem workshop," said one of the women haltingly.

"Oh, no. This is where the SAT class meets," said the man.

"I believe on our receipt it says room 108," another woman noted. I looked over at her. If you can stand up to a Marine, I'm sure you have higher self-esteem than I.

"Well, my kids have been using this room for three weeks already," said the man, spreading his class materials all over the desk at the front of the room. "Who are you people again?"

"The self-esteem class," a woman squeaked.

"I once taught a class on apathy," said the man, "but nobody showed up."

We were afraid that this wasn't a joke, so none of us laughed. A woman with a puffy face who appeared to be in her sixties decided it was time to take charge and called the Continuing Education office on her cell phone. After a few minutes of conversation, the woman announced, "We dysfunctionals will relocate to the room next door."

"My kids would beat you up if you stayed in here," said the Marine.

As we shuffled out of the room past the Marine, I wondered what he thought of us. I concluded that it was probably that we were a hopeless collection of unattractive slobs.

After several minutes, about fourteen of us, including, to my surprise, two decent looking men in their thirties, had congregated in the new room. If I had met these guys in any other setting, I never would have suspected that they had self-esteem issues. Men are so good at covering that up, while women, particularly depressed women, wear their moods on their sleeves.

Soon our instructor, a psychologist named Dr. Gerrie, flounced in. She was a vivacious and well put-together woman who radiated empathy.

"Welcome!" she enthused. "And congratulations on wanting higher self-esteem. It's definitely something you shouldn't leave home without."

Gerrie encouraged us to arrange ourselves in a semi-circle so that we couldn't hide behind our low self-esteem. "It takes a lot just to get to this seminar," she said, going through the class roster. "There were twenty-four of you signed up and look—only fourteen of you had the courage to show up. That's a very sad commentary, because low self-esteem is at epidemic proportions in our society."

I thought it was only an epidemic in my family.

Gerrie then took to the blackboard and scrawled "parenting by exception" across it. "Does anyone know what this means?"

"We want our children to like us?" said one woman carefully.

"It's related to that," said Gerrie. "The only feedback parents give is corrective or critical."

Well, certainly the feedback my parents gave was.

"Now, in my case," Gerrie continued, "I was the ne'er-do-well. As a result, I turned from a normal neurotic into a person who developed terrible phobias. I got into therapy when I was in my twenties and joined the self-esteem movement."

I was somewhat lost because I had never known there was a formalized "movement" to increase self-esteem, although if I had, my mother would probably have dismissed it as "some feminist horseshit."

While I was dwelling on more bad feelings about my mother, Gerrie scribbled on the chalkboard, "the looking glass self."

"What does this refer to?" she asked. Before anyone of us could respond, she answered her own question. "It's that when we are children, we think about who we are based on who our parents think we are."

Flashback: I'm ten years old in sleep-away camp. My parents are scheduled to take a vacation to Japan. The night before they are to leave I'm hysterically crying that I want to come home. "What are you trying to do to us?" my mother screeches over the telephone. "We've paid for this trip! What is the matter with you? We don't understand why you act up like this!"

Back to Gerrie: "Our parents were not psychotic or delusional. Our parents were normal neurotics. They loved us, but somehow they could not communicate that love."

Someone in the corner snorted.

My mother was Sybil (the title of a bestseller about a woman with multiple personalities many years ago), I wanted to say. Instead, I thought, I'm not so sure my parents loved me.

"We're a feeling-phobic society," Gerrie went on. "We're not supposed to have feelings. So when we have them, our parents are threatened by them and say they are 'wrong.' " Gerrie paused for effect and then said, "The root of all low self-esteem is the child's feeling that he or she is not loved enough."

Amen.

"Did you see that movie with Drew Barrymore where she divorced her parents?" one woman asked.

"Yes," said Gerrie, "*Irreconcilable Differences.*"

"She's a great role model," said another woman.

"I have a client who called her daughter ugh for *ugly*," said Gerrie.

"That's like my mother," said the woman.

I was somewhat amazed by these confessions. I wasn't aware that there could possibly be mothers out there who made their daughters feel any more imperfect than mine had. All the time my mother was apparently praising my accomplishments to others, she never once heaped praise on me to my face nor said anything nice to me about my personality or looks. Anytime I broached her lack of support, she cut the conversation short with a "Please. You're aggravating me." However, she had stopped short of calling me derogatory nicknames.

"The way we start to build self-esteem is to accept who we are in the moment," Gerrie announced. "It's the willingness to love ourselves." Feeling that this was a goal that would always be somewhat out of our reach, the class let out a collective sigh. Gerrie did not want us to feel exceptional in this regard, so she confessed to us that when she was nine, her mother had told her that she would marry at sixteen and become a prostitute by thirty.

We gasped.

"So you know what?" said Gerrie. "I got married at eighteen and I really started worrying. I developed claustrophobia and agoraphobia, and I wound up in the office of a therapist who was a European refugee and the most wonderful woman I had ever met."

Jeez, I thought. Is Gerrie as fucked up as I am? *Naw.*

Gerrie went on to tell us that Dr. Hauptman made her understand that anyone can develop a basic core of self-esteem. "We just have to learn that the things our parents told us about ourselves as children are outdated, distorted and obsolete. We can change our mind tapes."

I'll never be able to do that, I thought, imagining the alternative of strapping my mother to a medieval torture instrument.

After we had somewhat broken the ice by going around the room introducing ourselves, Gerrie told us that she wanted us to pair up and participate in an exercise. She told us to take a pen and paper and stated, "Let's get all the yuckies out. Answer these questions:

"I have low self-esteem because …

"I would have higher self-esteem if …

"I can increase my self-esteem by …

"Describe your mother with three adjectives.

"Describe your father with three adjectives.

"Write one thing you have learned from each parent that has not helped you and one thing from each parent that has helped you.

"Write ten things you love about yourself."

I will need about three weeks for that, I thought.

I quickly put pen to paper and was on the verge of writing something like, "My parents abandoned me when I was three and I was raised by wolves. Though they taught me wilderness survival, they knew nothing about manners, so when I was reintroduced to humans at age twenty-one, I was considered a slovenly mess and nobody wanted to be my friend. Half wolf, half human, I never fit in anywhere." At the last minute, I changed my mind and wrote about the feelings of resentment I had for my family.

When we were done with the exercise, Gerrie reported that we now had a composite picture of our lives. "I'm going to read my answers first to give you an idea of how I perceive myself," she said. Gerrie proceeded to go through a laundry list of her deficiencies. "I'm lazy, undisciplined, overweight, weird, bossy, self-centered and greedy," she said.

Is that all? I wanted to joke.

Gerrie moved down the list of questions and got to her mother, whom she described as "only concerned with looks" and "flirty," and her father, whom she referred to as "intellectual, unhappy and distant."

After Gerrie was finished, she must have realized that we were aghast, because she quickly added, "Remember, everything we say here is in confidence. I don't need you to go around telling everyone, 'You know that Dr. Gerrie Moran? She's a therapist and she's all screwed up.'"

There was a smattering of nervous laughter.

But you *are* all screwed up, I thought. That's probably why you became a therapist. My God, what if Isabel is all screwed up, too? What if she's a pedophile, or worse yet, moonlights as a real estate broker? Then I realized that I was catastrophizing again.

"Now," continued Gerrie, breaking my reverie, "I want you to share your responses with the person sitting next to you."

We immediately fell silent.

"Just pretend you're in a dear friend's living room, offering 'unconditional positive regard' and being completely non-judgmental."

That's impossible for me, I thought. I always made the harshest judgments about myself, but I was also especially fond of making pronouncements about whether other people were good or bad. This included rating them on everything from how they played tennis to how they raised their children.

Queasily, I looked at the girl sitting to my left. She seemed to be in her early thirties and was casually dressed in jeans and sneakers. I felt a tenuous rapport with her, so I smiled at her and she smiled back. "Do you want to go first?" she asked me.

"Sure," I said and began to systematically make my confessions. I told my sharing partner that I had low self-esteem because my parents had been highly critical, judgmental and negative with me and that they had constantly undermined me, even if they were unaware that they were doing so, and that they hadn't loved me for who I was, and they were constantly trying to remake me, and so on and so forth. When I finally looked up, I could see that the girl's mouth was agape. Clearly, my brutal honesty was much more than she had bargained for in coming to the class.

"Well," she said. "Well."

"I'm wrong," I said immediately. "I didn't answer the questions correctly. I'm sorry. It's all my fault."

Flashback: I say something evil to my sickly older brother and he says something even more evil back. I cry. My father says, "Wendy, it's all your fault because you started it."

Back to class: "No, no, no," my partner said, trying to comfort me. "You were fine."

"Now it's time for your partner to go," Gerrie announced.

As the girl went through her answers, I could hardly hear what she was saying. Here I had confessed my deepest, darkest family secrets and self-loathing to a complete stranger, who most likely thought I was only one notch removed from the homeless lady from my Winning Ways class. I heard snippets here and there, things like "I beat my depression by working out regularly at a gym," "I lost fifty pounds" and "I'm in therapy," but the fact that my partner was a lot like me never really penetrated for very long. To make matters worse, by the end of her monologue I had also added "terrible listener" to the list of things I hated about myself.

"All right, now," Gerrie interjected after a few more minutes. "Did we find out that we're not all that different?"

But what if you still feel different? I wanted to ask. Do you need to go into a remedial self-esteem class?

"Now I want each of you to put that wagging finger in your pocket," Gerrie continued. "You know the one I'm talking about. The self-critic."

It's not a finger for me. It's more like ten fingers.

"And I also want you to accept your dark side. Self-esteem building means giving yourself a realistic assessment of your strengths and weaknesses and accepting your weaknesses."

But what if all you see are weaknesses?

The rest of the class seemed skeptical as well, so Gerrie proclaimed that we were now going to have a twenty-minute open forum during which everyone would have the opportunity to discuss anything they felt was relevant. At first there was dead silence filled in slightly by Gerrie's expansive smile.

"What should we say?" a mousy-looking woman asked.

"Whatever you would like," said Gerrie, staring, I felt, directly at me.

Finally, the puffy woman who had led the charge to the new classroom said, "We probably all have the same types of insecurities. It spans generations."

My insecurities are worse than your insecurities, so there!

Gerrie nodded knowingly and stared at me again. I said nothing

"I was introduced to the concept of self-esteem in religious school," volunteered my sharing partner. "There was a chapter on it in a book we had. So I went up to the teacher and I asked what self-esteem was, and he said it was 'you.'"

"Was that helpful?" Gerrie asked sympathetically.

"Not exactly," said my partner. "By the time I got to the twelfth grade, I still did not have a concept of who I was."

But at least you have enough self-confidence to confess this.

"I'm fifty and I don't know who I am or what I want to be when I grow up," a woman spoke up. This was followed by some more nervous laughter. I looked around and noted that everyone seemed to be a bit more relaxed. Everyone but me. I was terrified that Gerrie was going to call on me. She gazed in my direction again, but before I knew it, another woman spoke. "I think we took more of the weaknesses away from our parents rather than the strengths," she said.

"That's interesting you should note that," said Gerrie, looking at me again.

"My mother always told me not to make waves," said one of the guys in the class. "So I always followed the path of least resistance. I just totally denied my feelings."

I should say that things were that way in my family, too, I thought, but I was too afraid to contribute it.

Again I felt Gerrie staring at me, and I shifted awkwardly in my seat.

"I never had anything negative directed at me by my parents," the puffy woman volunteered. "I don't get it. I had an exceptional marriage and good friends. So how did I get this low self-esteem?"

I detected a sneer developing on Gerrie's lips, and she looked like she wanted to pounce on the puffy woman, but she said nothing. Then she gazed in my direction again.

"My parents didn't say anything negative to me, but they expected me to become a doctor or a lawyer and I didn't do either," a blonde woman near me piped up. "They were perfectionists, so I applied that to myself."

"Let's continue with the 'I' statements," announced Gerrie.

I'm such a perfectionist, I can't even come up with an "I" statement because I'm afraid it will not live up to my own standards.

"I'm glad I came here today," said one woman.

"When I'm by myself, I'm okay," said another. "But when I'm in a relationship, my self-esteem caves in. I can't take any confrontations."

"I'll be in a situation," said one of the guys, "and I'll want to say something, and I don't. And then the next day, I'll snap."

People came up with their confessions one by one. The only one who didn't contribute was me, and I was acutely aware that Gerrie knew it.

"I'm a cop, and as soon as I take off my badge and gun, I become a wimp," said a woman with a deep voice and short red hair.

"I'm a lawyer, and people can't understand why I don't know how to express myself," said the other guy in the class.

On and on it went, as I felt myself becoming more and more conspicuous by virtue of my non-participation. I felt that every time Gerrie said something, she was somehow commenting on me. In an effort, I felt, to get me to contribute, Gerrie even started throwing her own two cents in. "I got a Ph.D. at forty and my mother didn't come to the ceremony," she said. "She didn't come to my wedding, either."

I tried to understand why I wasn't contributing. I remembered once reading that we are like cars and self-esteem is like oil. Even when the oil is running low, most cars have a reservoir of it to lubricate the car's engine and keep it running smoothly. Depressives, however, have no such self-esteem reservoir. Thus, making any kind of confession similar to ones my classmates were coming out with could threaten to permanently break me down.

Mercifully, after several more minutes of group therapy, Gerrie applauded our candor and told us that we were going to take a half-hour lunch break. Cognizant that I did not merit applause, I darted out the door as fast as I could, bought a soda in a vending machine and sat in a corner in the hallway, nibbling on my turkey sandwich and sipping my drink. I often found unstructured social situations like this terrifying and always tended to isolate when I encountered them. Now I noticed that several of my classmates were coalescing in groups to chat. This sent shivers down my spine because once again I felt like an outsider.

Flashback: my father is undergoing open-heart surgery and my mother, two brothers and I are in the lobby of the hospital waiting for word. The surgeon comes in and tells us that everything went smoothly and that my father is in recovery. My mother and brothers embrace. I stand a few feet away. Alone. They do not notice.

Back to class: After I finished my lunch, I made my way back to the classroom and took my seat. My sharing partner sat in her chair, eating her own sandwich.

"What gym do you belong to?" I asked her, feeling compelled to say something.

"Bally's in Rockville Centre," she replied.

"Oh, I belong to New York," I said.

"That's great," my partner said.

"Yeah," I said, "but I only go once a month for twenty minutes." My partner looked at me quizzically. No one gets my sense of humor. "How often do you go?" I asked.

"I used to go every night," she said, "but now I'm down to four nights a week."

"That's wonderful," I said, feeling totally inadequate. "Do you work full-time?"

"Yes," my partner said. "I'm a photographer for the Town of Lakeview."

"Oh, that must be fun," I replied.

"Not when you have to go ask people who don't like one another to stand next to each other for a photo," she said.

"That could be difficult," I said, picturing it. And I could. If there was one thing I had, it was radar for other people's emotions.

"And the Hasidic Jews are the worst," she said. For the first time I noticed that my partner was wearing a small cross. My heart pounded as I expected the next word out of her mouth to be some variation of the word *kike*. Even if she was going to utter this epithet, however, I didn't know if I had the courage to tell her that I, myself, was Jewish.

"You know why it's terrible?" she said. "They don't think women should work, so when they see me, they walk right in front of the camera while I'm trying to take shots."

"Yes, I can see them doing that," I said, not knowing how to respond.

At this point, Gerrie came back into the room and placed her business cards, tapes, books and flyers on the desk. "There are some things I have up here that you might be interested in after class," Gerrie proclaimed as everyone filtered back into the classroom. When we had reconvened, Gerrie noticed that there was one person missing. "Who is it?" she wanted to know.

"It's Gloria," said one of my classmates.

"You see," said Gerrie, without completing her thought. "All of you should congratulate yourselves for having the courage to complete this class."

So I'm completing the class. Big deal.

Then Gerrie distributed a handout to each of us, entitled, "Clues to Recognizing Your Self-Esteem." On one side was a list with the header, "High Self-Esteem." It had a list of attributes of those who felt good about themselves, ranging from "proud of accomplishments" to "approaches new challenges enthusiastically." I duly noted that I exhibited none of these attributes.

I eagerly waited for Gerrie to tell me how I might go about getting these attributes, but she was pontificating on the idea that we all need something called "connectiveness."

"We can act independently without being isolative like the Marlboro Man," she pointed out. "If he was so great, he wouldn't have died of lung cancer."

"If he had high self-esteem, he wouldn't have smoked," said one of my classmates.

I reached for the nicotine patch I had placed on my back that morning. Many depressives I had met in the psychiatric hospital smoked, and I had been doing it on and off since I was a teenager. Like most addicts, I usually partook every time an uncomfortable emotion rose to the surface of my psyche. Intellectually, I knew it was a deadly habit and had been trying unsuccessfully to quit.

"What ever happened to the Marlboro Man's horse?" another person now asked.

"He probably had poor self-esteem, too," said another.

After she had gone over the remaining points in the handout, Gerrie apparently felt it was time to revisit the puffy woman's assertion that she had no idea where she had gotten her low self-esteem from. "Where do we get low self-esteem from?" asked Gerrie. Before anyone could reply she said, "It doesn't come from the inside. Assertiveness is your birthright. Look at babies. They fall down and they get right up and try again. They don't fall down and say, 'I guess I'm no good at this, so I should stop.'"

Looking somewhat chastised, the puffy woman said, "What if you are emotionally attached to toxic people?"

"You have to get rid of them," said Gerrie.

I pictured sending certain people I had known out into the Atlantic in a rowboat with no life preservers.

Gerrie continued. "You should surround yourself with people who don't 'should' on your feelings. In other words, people who tell you that you 'shouldn't' feel a certain way when you *do* feel that way."

"How can you deal with someone who is negative, though?" the puffy woman continued, beginning to cry.

"You tell them, 'Please do not should on my feelings,' or, if you can't do that, engage in free writing about them and then rip it up so no one can see it."

"But…" said the puffy woman.

"You have to act as if you have self-esteem," continued Gerrie, "and you can begin to act as if you value yourself by wearing nice underwear."

"How did you know my underwear is ripped?" the puffy woman said, weeping. I was amazed that she had enough self-esteem oil in her system to make these admissions freely to a group of people she had never met before.

"I went to the store and bought sixty-secen dollars' worth of underwear," said Gerrie, trying to stop the tears. "Then I said to myself, 'How can you spend sixty-seven dollars on underwear when there are children wearing burlap sacks?' I don't know what the solution is."

"Don't wear underwear," said one of the guys in the class.

The puffy woman laughed.

After a short bathroom break we returned and Gerrie continued on the decent-underwear kick. "You have to ask yourself what you can do for the little girl inside," she said. "If you change your behavior by engaging in little acts of self-care, then your attitude will change, too."

Where's the best place to buy good underwear? I wanted to ask. Instead, I thought about how I rarely engaged in acts of self-care. I almost never got manicures or pedicures, took bubble baths or got massages. Maybe I just felt like I wasn't worth it.

Gerrie randomly spewed sound bites of wisdom. "Appreciate from where you come," she said. "Appreciate your uniqueness. Don't compare yourself to others. Remember, nobody knows what you've been through better than you."

I was still thinking about my pathetic underwear collection when Gerrie distributed another handout. This one had two columns. On one side it said "Power" and under it, "Inner Directed." In the other column the heading was "No Power" and beneath it, "Outer Directed."

"I want you to go down these lists and check every statement that's relevant to you," Gerrie directed us.

It only took a few seconds for me to determine that I largely had No Power. The only statement I checked in the "Power" column was "able to be vulnerable when safe." I was frightened to death when Gerrie instructed us to share with our partners which items we had checked. I glanced over at the worksheet of the girl sitting next to me and saw that she had several "Power" statements checked.

"I … I only have one item checked," I croaked. *I've totally failed this class too.*

"That's okay," said the girl.

"Now I want each of you who checked at least three items in the "Power" column to raise your hands," said Gerrie. The hands of most of the people in the room shot up. Gerrie looked squarely at me and stated, "That's okay, Wendy."

My heart pounded and I wanted to run for the hills. Our instructor now knew that I needed remedial a self-esteem class. Either that or she was making a bid to be my therapist. I figured Gerrie knew that I was already in therapy, so I was convinced that she believed I needed two therapists.

"I'm so embarrassed," I told my partner.

"I bet you could have checked off more," she volunteered.

"You have high self-esteem," I told her.

"No, I don't," she said. "Just the other day, I was at this McDonald's and I saw this van full of blind people pull up. The two handicapped spots were taken illegally, so the driver had nowhere to park. I went into the restaurant and told the manager about it, but he didn't want to do anything."

"What does that have to do with you?" I asked.

"I should have stood up on the counter and announced that whoever illegally parked in the handicapped spot should move his car, but I didn't do anything."

"Most people wouldn't," I replied.

"But doesn't that show that I have low self-esteem?"

"I think it shows you have a brain," I said. "You could have been yelling at a three-hundred-pound construction man to move his car. And then where would you have been?"

"I guess you're right," she said. "But you know what else? This girl who works out at the gym with me asked me to go dancing with some of her friends and I said I couldn't go."

"Do you like dancing?" I asked.

"No," she said.

"Then I don't know why you should feel that you had to go," I said. After a moment I added, "Oh, my God. I'm shoulding on your feelings. I'm terribly sorry." *Thank God Gerrie's not grading me!*

"No, I'm sorry," she said.

"No, I'm the one to blame," I responded.

At this point, Gerrie distributed another handout called "Five

Conditions of Self-Esteem." The conditions included "belonging," "uniqueness," "models and mentors," "personal power and accomplishments," and "risks." This last one especially caught my eye. It said,

> Risk is a necessary factor of good mental health, but can also result in failure. Yet a life without risk is a life without opportunity for accomplishment.

I remembered that after my first hospitalization, Dr. Trieste urged me to take risks. He didn't mean major, monumental risks. Just small risks. Like having a party or inviting a friend over for dinner. I had tried to follow his advice, and it always made me feel a little bit better about myself.

"According to Robert Frost, the best way out of something is through it," Gerrie now told us. "We have to be careful of avoiding something simply because it's uncomfortable when the end result is something we want. On the other hand," she added, "life is not about struggle either."

"How can you tell if it's something you want, or something that is not right for you?" asked the guy lawyer. "I prefer to write briefs and motions and hate going to trial. Now, is that something I'm afraid of, or something that is just not right for me?"

"That's a very tough question," said Gerrie, retrieving one of her business cards from the desk and handing it to him. He stuck it in his wallet as Gerrie handed out the final worksheet, entitled "Ideal Self." Underneath the heading was a box containing the word "Accept" and an arrow pointing down. Beneath it was a box with the word "Risk" and an arrow pointing up.

"Your self-esteem is dependent on the degree to which your real and ideal selves come together," said Gerrie. "The gap between the two is called 'the Misery Gap.'"

My gap is as wide as the earth's distance from the moon.

Gerrie instructed us to write down a set of acceptable risks or "esteemable actions" that we could realistically achieve, thereby closing our misery gap. I quickly wrote down, "exercise more and lose weight" and "socialize more and meet a guy I'd like to date." I wrote a few smaller risks and looked up at Gerrie triumphantly. For a moment I thought she was going to hand me her card without my even asking for it. But she just smiled back.

When I got home, I began to synthesize. In a class full of people who thought they had low self-esteem, my low self-esteem was the outright champion. None of these people, I was sure, had ever sat across from a psychiatrist and told him exactly how she was going to kill herself, as I had. Not one of them, I was sure, had ever gone into a total tailspin when someone told them something unflattering about their personality, as I routinely did. As far as I was concerned, they were low self-esteem dilettantes.

At the same time, Dr. Gerrie had managed to hit something deep within me, something almost totally destroyed, which said there was hope for me yet. All I had to do was try to take those "esteemable actions," those little risks that led to the closing of the Misery Gap—the difference between who you thought you were and who you wanted to be. It made perfect sense to me, but was it truly possible?

In the mail that evening, I found a letter from my healthcare provider, which promoted a health line that you could call twenty-four hours a day. Since I decided there and then that being fitter would be one small step toward closing my Misery Gap, I called the hotline and chose "Developing Your Personal Fitness Plan" from the options. At the same time, I realized that depression is the catch-22 of illnesses in that the very things that allow us to recover from it are the things we find hardest to do. One of those was exercise—a great depression breaker. But I was often filled with lethargy and an overwhelming feeling that a walk around the block was as insurmountable a task as ascending Mount Everest.

"It seems like there are dozens of reasons to work out," a man's voice on the hotline said. "Why is it so easy to become a fitness dropout when fitness offers wonderful health benefits?" The man went on to say that a personal fitness plan might be the missing part of the equation.

"Aha," I said to myself.

"Let's do a personal attitude check," said the man. "Are negative feelings associated with exercise?"

Yes.

"Is shame, embarrassment or guilt associated with starting and sticking with a fitness program?"

"Definitely," I said to the man's voice.

"Does exercise feel like a chore?" the voice asked.

"Yes!" I stated emphatically to the voice. "The first five minutes on my recumbent bike is more torturous than cleaning my blinds."

"Are you too busy to exercise?" asked the voice.

"Yes! I'm on a job that sucks the life out of me for eight hours a day," I reported to the voice.

"Do you feel guilty when you don't exercise?" the voice continued.

"God, yes," I cried.

"One activity may be pleasurable to one person and grueling to another person," the voice explained.

"Any activity is grueling," I told the voice.

"Substantial health benefits can be gained simply by fitting moderate amounts of physical activity into your day," said the voice, which went on to recommend doing traditional chore-oriented activities. "Make it enjoyable and part of your lifestyle," the voice said. "Allow exercise to nurture your body, not punish it."

The voice went on to tell me to set realistic short- and long-term goals, focus on the progress, not the end result, and gauge my progress by the healthful habits I am adopting rather than the numbers on the scale. He also said to stop the *should-do*'s and do what is right for me. "Think positive thoughts about yourself such as 'I will' and 'I can.' Above all, choose exercise and physical activities that you enjoy."

After the man's diatribe was over, I hung up the phone and decided that my regimen would begin immediately. The next day was Saturday and I made a point of getting down on my hands and knees and cleaning my kitchen floor (I'm opposed to mops) and bathtub. My cat looked on quizzically, as these were activities that she seldom saw me engaged in.

"Isn't this fun?" I asked her. "I'm just having so much fun. I will. I can," I said. My cat gave me a disinterested look and licked her ass. Then, apparently overcome by the smell of cleaning fluids, she puked. Fortunately, this was yet another opportunity for me to get down on my hands and knees and clean.

I knew the big test would come when I returned to a regular workday, and sure enough, that Monday I got two pieces of bad news during the day with regard to my writing. First, emissaries from the marketing department were not satisfied with some creative writing concepts I submitted and wanted me to come up with something new.

"What exactly are you looking for?" I asked.

"You know," the woman told me. "More."

"More of what?" I inquired.

"You know," she said, gesturing in circular motions with her hands. "Just *more.*"

Then, when I got home that evening, I found a rejection letter from a small niche publisher for a book I had written. The letter led me to believe that I couldn't create anything more interesting than a shopping list. I should just kill myself and be done with it, I thought. But then, what will happen to my cat?

So I thought about my personal exercise plan. "I can, I will," I said to my cat, who yawned in my face. I got on my recumbent bike and pedaled.

Chapter 4

Singled Out

"You do come up with some doosies," said an astonished Isabel when I told her that I was going to participate in an evening of Speeddating, the way for Jewish singles to meet. It was most likely dreamed up by a sadistic married rabbi.

What was she saying? That I was a total freak? Yes, that's what I decided she was saying.

"Why do you think it's so strange?" I asked defensively. Of course, like most depressives, I had a very thin skin and was always on the lookout for signs of disapproval, especially from my therapist.

"I think it's great," countered Isabel.

"Dr. Gerrie said that she goes with a lump in her throat, but she goes." I continued.

My therapist looked threatened. "Does Dr. Gerrie have literature?" she asked sharply.

"Yes," I snapped. "I'll bring it to you at our next session."

When I got home from my therapy session, I plopped down on my couch, my cat beside me. I could keep my little world the way it was, coming home every night to her, and like my cat, never grow. But wasn't that what being human was all about? If you didn't take a risk on the romantic front, how did you ever learn who you were meant for, or even who you were? And it wasn't like you had to secure a date with the Prince of Monaco to feel like you had accomplished something. No. Progress could come with the smallest of actions.

No one called me that night, so I spent most of it on my couch, listening to music. Except for a call from my building superintendent about the lack of heat in my apartment, I couldn't remember the last time I had actually spoken on the phone to a man who wasn't a relative. It was time to act.

So on the appointed evening I got dressed in black and applied makeup the way Barbara from Winning Ways had advised. As Dr. Gerrie had instructed, I tried to leave my self-critic in my apartment and I arrived at the Jewish Y, where the event was to be held, with what felt like a beach ball in my throat. Isabel was right. This is for losers. I'm here so I must be a loser too. I should just leave, I thought.

It was a sad fact of my depressive life that, as much as I craved a connection with members of the opposite sex, my actions usually left me isolated and alone. After all, I subconsciously reasoned, it was much better to reject a person before he had the opportunity to reject me. When I lived in Los Angeles in my twenties, I was a pro at this. I rejected men because I didn't like the way they smelled, or laughed, or drove a car, or—you name it. I had a reason to reject them. It got to the point where friends just rolled their eyes when I told them what was wrong with a particular guy.

I did become involved with a few men in Los Angeles, but I waited to do that until I made absolutely, positively, unreservedly sure that they were THE WRONG MEN. And, of course, there were the many men I pined over who would never have me, which was very convenient for someone who feared being in a relationship altogether.

When I returned to New York, I met a man who was a writer. While he was the first man I had dated who was not a candidate for intensive psychoanalysis, he did have several undesirable qualities, like being cheaper than plastic beads and farting during intercourse. I wasn't in love with him and knew we could never be married.

At this point, my mother screamed at me, "Eliot wants to go out with you. Who else are you going to find who could deal with your history of depression?"

So I became engaged to Eliot. Later, Isabel gave me permission to end the relationship, which I did. But my mother's words had hit home, and I became convinced that I would never find anybody.

Somewhere along the way, I had also come to know that women who have good relationships with their fathers have no problem finding an emotionally healthy man to love and be loved by, while those of us whose relationships were problematic were lost in the wilderness. I classified myself in the latter category—I never knew how much my father loved me because he never expressed his love to me. Instead, he did things like tell me how fabulous the women who worked at the hospital where he was undergoing cardiac rehab were.

"They are so friendly and cheerful," he would say to me. "You should be a little more like them."

The only time I ever heard my father say something loving, even to my mother, was the night before he died.

With the help of Isabel, however, I finally felt like I had some idea of what to look for in a man. The only problem was that there were far fewer men to choose from now that I was in my late thirties than there had been in my twenties. This called for drastic measures.

"Hi!" chirped Ellen, the singles coordinator at the SpeedDating sign-in table. It has come to this, I thought.

"Put your name tag on and read the rules." She handed me a brochure with the title *SpeedDating Participant Kit*. As I struggled to get the adhesive part of my name tag exposed, I glanced past the sign-in table. I was in a large recreation room with a sizable wooden Jewish star and DJ equipment in one corner (most likely for use at some mutant Bat Mitzvah). About twelve bridge tables with numbered place cards on them sat a few feet apart from each other. At some, a man and a woman engaged in strained conversation. Others had just one member of either sex. "You're at table five," clucked Ellen.

As I made my way to table five, I realized that I would be sitting at the table alone for now. I got a closer look at some of the participants. The men mostly looked pensive or bemused. One man seemed to be leering at me, but then he appeared to lapse into a coma. The women looked stricken. As I tried to size up my competition, I wondered how many of them had good relationships with their fathers. Probably none if they had to resort to SpeedDating.

I sat down at my table, picked up my rules kit and date card and started reading. I didn't like the rules, so I made up my own including:

Please do not spit, sneeze or drool on your date.

Please do not ask your date where he stands on stem cell research.

Please do not ask your date if he will remember your anniversary.

Please do not ask your date where he clips his toenails.

Please do not ask your date when the last time he spoke to his mother was.

Please do not ask your date whether he prefers to take magazines or newspapers into the john.

Please do not ask your date if he will share the TV remote with you.

In order to avoid making eye contact with anyone, I kept my eyes focused on the rules long after I had finished reading them. I looked up after several minutes and saw a blubbery, unnaturally blonde woman who appeared to be in her fifties at the sign-in table. She wore a skintight black tank top and pedal pushers, which served only to accentuate her thick rolls of fat. Moments later she made her way to the bridge table next to mine. Sitting there was a slick-looking man dressed in a natty gray suit and black loafers. As Blubber sat across from him, he looked as horrified as, say, a man who had been quite literally asked to eat shit. She ignored this and immediately made conversation. "I signed up for two of these events this week," she told him.

"This will be my last," he said.

"Can I have everyone's attention," announced Ellen. "I'm going to explain how this evening is going to work."

Ellen went on to tell us that we would get seven minutes to talk to the member of the opposite sex sitting across from us. At the end of seven minutes, Ellen would strike her triangle and the men would each move two tables down and begin again with their new dates. This would go on until all the men and women in the room had had a chance to talk to each other.

"I'm so glad I'm not rotating," Blubber said to her first date.

"There are two more women than men," Ellen explained, "so two women will sit out for each date." All I could think was: I want to sit out for every date. There is no one here who can heal the tremendous hurt I feel inside. But Ellen struck her triangle and said, "Go."

The men and women who were seated together began to engage in conversation again. I eavesdropped on Blubber and heard little snippets of the conversation like "How long have you been single?" and "My husband was well until he got sick."

After several minutes Ellen tapped her triangle. The man sitting across from Blubber looked as relieved as someone who has just found out that he has beaten cancer.

"Now, each man moves two tables," said Ellen. "So if you're at table five, you go to table seven."

A man named Lane, who looked like a frog in glasses, approached and sat down at my table. I instantly knew that this was going to be painful. He did not seem inclined to kick off the conversation, so I began instead. "Have you done this before?" I asked him.

"Yes, I've done it twice before," he said.

"Did you like it?" I followed up.

"I chose sixteen women and none of them picked me," he said.

"Oh, I'm sorry," I said, not having an inkling of how to comfort the man.

"No, that's not right," he said. "One woman chose me but she was compulsively religious."

"Oh, my," I said.

"It's the women who have all the power in this," he went on. "They get to choose who they want to go out with."

"But you get to choose, too," I interjected.

"I think every woman is looking for the last great man," he said. Then he beamed as though he had just said something deeply profound.

"Well, I'm not," I said in a small voice.

"All these divorced women have all these stories of what this one did to her and what that one did to her. I don't have any of these stories because I'm widowed."

"Oh, I'm sorry," I said. "When did your wife pass away?"

"Three years ago," said Lane, his eyes misting over.

"Oh, I'm so sorry," I repeated. Suddenly, I began to feel consumed by Lane's sorrow.

Flashback: My mother finds out that my sickly older brother has to go into the hospital for another surgery. She starts crying as she tells me. She is sullen and doesn't speak the rest of the night. There is nothing I can do to comfort her. I am useless. I want to tell her that a teacher at school spoke to me sharply and hurt my feelings. I don't because I realize it's not the right time. It is never the right time to tell my mother about my feelings.

Back to Lane: He was weeping. The only thing I could do was pray for the sound of Ellen's triangle.

"She had a genetic defect," Lane said of his wife. "Men can have it and live with it for twenty-five years, but women get it and they're gone."

"Oh, that's terrible," I said again, feeling more and more sad. *You're eating me up with your problems.*

For the entire rest of our time together, Lane repeatedly told me that nobody wanted to date him. "You see, I'll pick you," said Lane, flourishing his pen and showing me that he was checking the box that said, "I would like to see this person again." "But you ..." his voice trailed off.

Never mind the sixteen other women who had rejected Lane; at this point, I felt like I was totally responsible for his misery. Thankfully, a few minutes later, Ellen's triangle chimed and Lane was gone. In his place came a tall, thin bald man named Dick, who greeted me warmly. I began the conversation by telling him that this was my first time SpeedDating and that I was a little nervous.

"Oh, it's much better than any other method, especially since they don't have Jewish dances anymore."

"I know. Isn't it terrible?" I agreed emphatically although I had never been to a Jewish dance.

"Yeah, well, it's tough to meet people at our age," he said.

"Are you divorced?" I asked Dick.

"No, widowed."

This is just my luck. "Oh, really. I'm sorry," I said.

"We moved out to the suburbs with the boys and six months later she was gone."

At this moment, I felt compelled to introduce Dick to Lane, but then I realized that both of them had probably already met their share of widowers in bereavement groups. Still, I wondered how I could repair Dick. In another clear sign that I had no boundaries, I felt like it was my duty to make him happy. That's why for the next six minutes, I let Dick talk about his three boys and their extracurricular activities, and about how his wife's family hadn't helped at all with their upbringing, but how his parents had been there for him.

"Some single women can accept a man with kids," he said, looking at me suspiciously. "Some can't."

"I know," I said. *And count me in that latter category.*

"How many kids do you have?" Dick wanted to know.

"None," I said.

Dick looked away to indicate that our conversation was decidedly over. It occurred to me that neither Dick nor Lane had allowed me to express my sorrows. But even if they had, I doubt I would have said very much—I was too afraid. Perhaps, like my mother, they wouldn't consider my sorrows particularly interesting or important.

I proceeded to go through three more dates. I didn't meet any more widowers, just bitter divorcees. At the end of the evening I met Tony, the guy who had originally been sitting across from Blubber. Tony and I hit if off immediately.

"I love your sleeves," he told me.

I appreciated the compliment because I was particularly enamored of my jacket's sleeves. Although it was forbidden, we talked about our respective careers. He, it turned out, was a talk-radio host who had to write a lot of his own material.

"Don't you love writing?" he asked me.

"Yes," I replied, overjoyed that I had met someone with the same interests.

In a brief lull in the conversation, I noted that Tony was wearing a sweater under his suit jacket. "Aren't you hot?" I asked. "It's ninety degrees out."

"My respiratory system is different than most people's," he said. "The trick is to breathe through your nose, not your mouth."

I must have looked bewildered because Tony quickly changed the topic to what types of movies we liked. When the triangle chimed, I made a notation that I would like to see Tony again. Had I missed signs that he was another weirdo?

At the end of the evening, Ellen told us that if we had "a match" (in other words, a man and a woman who wanted to see each other again), she would contact us by phone the following day. I anxiously called in for my messages the next day and at 3:30 I got one from Ellen saying that I had a match with Tony and giving me his home and work phone numbers. I was thrilled, but not for too long. In my life, good news stuck with me for a nanosecond, while bad news hounded me for years.

"This sounds very promising," said my friend Joan when I told her what had transpired.

"If I get a boyfriend, I'll have to shave my legs several more times a week," I noted.

"Here she goes," said Joan. "Always the downside."

"That's what depressed people do," I insisted.

Tony called over the weekend and left a message. Realizing that we were now engaged in the game of appearing to have full lives without each other, I waited several hours to return his call, at which point he wasn't in. He called me back later that night, but I was high on post–dental work Vicodin and didn't pick up the phone. I called Tony the following evening and he wasn't home, so I left a message saying he could call me back until 10 p.m. At 9:55 p.m. he called.

"How was your weekend?" I asked him.

"Oh, terrible," he replied. "I was interviewing marketing people and it was like spending two days in Hitler's death camps."

"Oh, really?" I said, starting to worry. I always hated when non-Jews referred to the Holocaust because I feared that deep down they were all closet Nazi sympathizers.

"Do you know any marketing people?" Tony asked.

"No," I said. "Why do you need one?"

"It's for my radio show," said Tony.

"Yes, you said you were a radio show host," I responded. "What station are you on?"

"I'm on the Internet," Tony answered. "And I work part-time for my parents' metal refinishing company."

"Oh," I said, the picture suddenly becoming clearer. Tony was simply another entertainment industry wannabe, about as genuine as a penny stock tip.

"How's your agent?" Tony asked.

Had I told him about my agent? "He's still British," I said.

"Is he looking to promote a radio show?"

"I–I don't know," I stuttered, stunned by Tony's shamelessness.

"If he picks me up, I'll cut you in on the profits," Tony said.

"Uh-huh," I said. The rest of the conversation was a blur, although I did seem to recall Tony asking if he could pay my doctor brother under the table to write him a prescription for nasal allergy spray.

"Do you believe this?" I asked my friend Varteny the next day.

"You have to keep going," she said.

That night I ruminated about a crush I was developing on my agent, who was inconveniently married and lived an ocean away. I had seen his photo on his Web site and had been instantly smitten. As so often happens with me, my thoughts turned obsessive until Varteny, like a good friend, gently offered me a dish of reality. "He's not, you know. He's not ..."

"Available?" I said.

"Yes," she said. "And he lives, he lives …"

"In England?" I said.

"Yes," she replied.

"So what's your point?" I asked.

One thing I can never be accused of is not having a rich fantasy life. I have been falling for actors since I was a teenager. Maybe that comes from a fondness I have for emotionally remote men like my father.

That night, in the mail, I got a relationship profile questionnaire from Great Impressions, a national video dating company I had used many years before when I lived in Los Angeles. I had met a lot of men through the service and had rejected them all. I gave Great Impressions a call. A woman named Jennifer told me that the service was not cheap, but what we were talking about was an investment in my future and that I could come in virtually any time of the day or night because "love waits for no one."

Except me.

A little after dinnertime, I got a call from Tony. "My agent is only interested in books, not radio," I lied to him. "And I'm just about to go out for dinner, so can I call you tomorrow?" I lied again.

"Sure," said Tony. "What time?"

"Between six and seven," I said nervously. *I'm such a coward.*

The following night, between six and seven, I was out to dinner with some girlfriends telling them about the psycho case I had met at SpeedDating. Because of my experience with Tony, I was also convinced that I would never meet a normal eligible man.

"If you don't get married straight out of college, you're sunk," said one of my friends. "All that's left are freaks."

My other friend and I somberly agreed.

I got home about nine o'clock. At ten, my phone rang. I knew instinctively not to answer it. When I checked my machine, there was a long message from Tony accusing me of not calling when I was supposed to and telling me that if I wanted to end our "relationship" now, he thought that that was really "bad." "I hope you're dead," he said. "No, I mean I hope you're not dead, but that you had some emergency."

I was going to do the lame thing and leave a message on Tony's machine the following day when he was not home, but I inhaled deeply and called him a few minutes later. His machine picked up. "The reason I didn't call you," I said slowly, "is because I'm really not interested in seeing you again for reasons I'd rather keep private. I hope you can respect that. Good luck with SpeedDating." After I hung up, I breathed a sigh of relief. Then I immediately felt like a wimp for not waiting to actually talk to Tony. But I told myself that he was so strange that he had probably been listening to my message without picking up the phone and was most likely an alien from another galaxy who would be returning there in a few days.

That Sunday, I found myself in the nearest office of Great Impressions, a place that reeked of artificiality. I sat across from a piranha named Sandy, who was about to chew me to pieces by talking about when she, as I, had lived in Los Angeles.

"So you were a member of Great Impressions then?" she said.

"Yes," I said.

"Then you know what we're all about," she said.

"I'm not ready to make any decisions about joining today," I noted.

"What's preventing you from making a decision?" asked Sandy, who more and more was looking to me like a computer-generated image. I often found it very difficult to make decisions. For me, even deciding what to order at a restaurant was as difficult as the choices

President Kennedy faced during the Cuban Missile Crisis.

"What is the cost of this service?" I asked Sandy.

"We give a first-time incentive," she said.

"What does that mean?" I queried.

"You don't know what that means?" Sandy practically snarled.

"No," I squeaked.

"How come you don't look excited?" she suddenly asked.

"Me?" I said, panicked.

"Yes," said Sandy. She glanced down at the questionnaire I had filled out.

"Well ..." I said.

Clearly, Sandy was the sort of toxic person that Dr. Gerrrie had talked about in the self-esteem class, but I had no idea how to get rid of her.

"Look. You're forty and you've never been married," she said. "What could possibly prevent you from doing this?" she asked.

"I've been burned by dating services in the past," I whimpered.

"By which one?" Sandy wanted to know. I coughed up the name of a dating service that had walked away with a handful of my money. "Well, we are not like them," stated Sandy. "We've been in business for twenty years."

"That might be ..." I said.

Sandy glanced down at my questionnaire again, looking to see what my income was. "Are you having financial difficulties?" she asked sharply.

"N-no," I stuttered, "but I need time..."

"You drove all the way here in the rain and I'm just wondering why," snapped Sandy.

"Well," I said. "Well, I just need to think about this." I knew I had to stall Sandy because I had also signed up for the self-help class that was supposed to give me the insights necessary to get into a relationship without having to resort to a dating service.

"Take as long as you want," said Sandy, abruptly standing up. "Call us or don't call us. We don't care."

"Fine," I said, and quickly fled the office.

God, you've just been rejected by a dating service, I thought when I got to my car. How pathetic is that?

Three days before my class, I got a message on my machine that it was being canceled. I frantically called the continuing ed school. "Why was the class canceled?" I asked breathlessly.

"I don't know," said the man on the phone.

"Did the instructor find her soul mate and move to Paris?"

"I don't think so," said the man evenly.

Does she know that I signed up for the class? Is that why she's canceling?

When I got home I was hysterical. I re-read the course description in the school's catalogue. I would no longer be able to: A) Attract the right man without the trickery and deception encouraged by many catch-a-husband guides; B) Clarify my own dreams and needs; C) Avoid wasting time on inappropriate men; D) Feel comfortable addressing key issues like kids, chores, money and sex; or E) Build a healthy marriage without sacrificing mutual respect, integrity and my true self.

I wasn't sure how I could live without all of the vital information conveyed in the canceled class. In despair, I turned to the Internet, where, wonder of wonders, I found a book called *Finding Your Soul Mate Using the Science of Numerology*. I ordered it immediately. When it came, however, it told me that as a number one, I was at my best when I functioned in an executive capacity in a corporate environment. It goes without saying that *Finding Your Soul Mate* went straight into the trash.

Undeterred, I returned to the Internet and typed in the words "relationship counseling." From there I got onto a Web site for Lang Associates, personal growth consultants based in Tyler, Texas, who advertised that they could help anyone find her soul mate. I e-mailed the owner, Denise Lang, to see if she had any seminars scheduled in New York. It turned out that she did not, but she was available for phone consultations for a fee of one hundred dollars an hour. What could be better than my own private soul mate consultant? I signed up for a half-hour conversation. In my enthusiasm, I neglected to ask what Denise's credentials were. Afterwards, I decided that it was probably best if I didn't know.

At the appointed hour, I intrepidly dialed Denise's phone number.

"Hi, Denise. It's Wendy," I said

"Ye-as," said Denise, effervescing to the point where she reminded me more of a Southern high school cheerleader than a high-powered consultant. "What questions do you have for me, Wen-deee?"

(What I said) "Well, I was wondering what exactly a soul mate relationship is."

(What I thought) I'm so clueless.

(What Denise said) "A soul relationship is where two people come together as equals for the purpose of spiritual, mental, emotional and physical growth. Now, a lot of people come to me and say, Isn't a soul mate a person you're destined to meet from another life? And I say, Not necessarily. All we know is that if you are not a healthy person now, you will not attract a healthy person, and if you get in a healthy relationship now and you're not healthy, you will do behaviors that destroy it."

(What Denise thought) Give me an *L*.

(What I said) "Oh, really? Is there any way to avoid that?"

(What I thought) *L.*

(What Denise said) "The best way, Wen-deee, is to do everything you can to learn about yourself and become a healthy partner. You have to become one hundred percent of what you want to attract. Most people don't take the time to read books and go to seminars and meetings or look at past relationships and see what worked and what didn't work."

(What Denise thought) Give me an *O.*

(What I said) "I'm doing my best to do this."

(What I thought) *O.*

(What Denise said) "Say you have a pattern of being attracted to emotionally unavailable men. That's life's way of telling you a part of you is emotionally unavailable. Because like attracts like."

(What Denise thought) Give me an *S.*

(What I said) "I am attracted to emotionally unavailable men."

(What I thought) *S.*

(What Denise said) "Say you're attracted to an emotionally unavailable man and he decides he really likes you. Usually when that happens, you'll run. Usually it reminds you of something in your childhood. Perhaps your mom or dad weren't emotionally open and were closed to you."

(What Denise thought) Give me an *E.*

(What I said) "Yes, my father was emotionally unavailable."

(What I thought) *E.*

(What Denise said) "Once you place an awareness on it, you've begun the healing process. Then you have to have the willingness to take the risk and get into relationships."

(What Denise thought) Give me an *R.*

(What I said) "I'm willing to do that. But now that I'm willing to act on that, there are no available men left because I'm, like, forty."

(What I thought) *R.*

(What Denise said) "The mind is so powerful, Wen-deee. When you sa-ay 'There are no men available,' that's all you're going to see. It's like getting a new car. If yew say yew want a Jeep, then all you see are Jeeps everywhere. If you go with 'All the men are gone,' then your mind is going to show you proof of that. Now you've got to create a new belief to replace the old one.

(What Denise thought) What's that spell?

(What I said) "You mean there are men?"

(What I thought) Loser!

(What Denise said) "There are me-en everywhere. Yawer bra-ain is just a computer, Wen-dee. And when you hear your bra-ain say these things, you have to flip flop it. You have to say, 'Cancel, cancel,' and just repeat to yourself phrases like, 'I meet potential soul mates in my town regularly.'"

(What Denise thought) Yew are a hopeless loser.

(What I said) "Thanks, Denise."

(What I thought) I am a hopeless loser.

(What Denise said) "There is a flow to life, Wen-dee. And the greatest thing that you can do is understand this, and that when it's time for something to happen, it's going to happen. There are no accidents out there."

(What Denise thought) Say, "Ay-em a hopeless loser" louder.

(What I said) "You think when the timing is right it'll happen?"

(What I thought) AY-EM A PATHETIC, HOPELESS LOSER.

(What Denise said) "You have to do what you need to do to be healthy and happy and then learn how to be happy by yourself, so that when you find that special person, you're happy with him or without him."

(What Denise thought) Yey-as. Yew are a pathetic, hopeless loser.

(What I said) "Denise, do you have a soul mate?"

(What I thought) Tell me no, please.

(What Denise said) "Aye had one for three years and it recently ended. Aye have no regrets."

(What Denise thought) Yew are not in my league.

(What I said) "Gee, you really are together. All I have is regrets."

At the end of our conversation, Denise did tell me that I could e-mail her with questions any time I wanted. "I'll send you a check for the consultation," I told her.

"Ohh-kayy," said Denise.

My office was located in an upscale suburban town where I could test Denise's theories, but the question was, where exactly should I situate myself? At a heavily trafficked intersection? As I'm sure Denise would have told me, there would definitely be a "flow" there, even if it just consisted of cars whizzing by. I opted instead for a less dangerous vantage point—a gym I belonged to that had a location down the block from work. I had read about women meeting their spouses at gyms, but since I had a tendency to moan in agony when working out, I had pretty much stopped going. I decided that in the name of love, it was time to put that behind me. So the next day at lunchtime, I headed over to the health club in town.

"Do you have recumbent bicycles?" I asked the peppy blonde at the front desk.

"What are they?" she asked.

I turned around and saw a row of recumbent bicycles.

"Never mind," I said and headed down to the women's locker room. I was surprised at how crowded it was with other women, probably all saying to themselves things like, "I meet potential soul mates in my town regularly." After I had changed, I made my way back out to the floor and got on what looked like a comfortable recumbent bike. I'm being the best I can be, I thought, just like Denise had advised.

A suave looking man dressed in a tailored shirt, khakis and loafers leaned against a nearby bike with his gym bag slung over his shoulder. I looked at his left hand and noticed a wedding band. You see? Every man you are interested in is married, I said to myself. Then, I quickly added Denise's "cancel, cancel."

About five minutes into my ride, I wasn't moaning, and I felt fairly certain that I was not going to expire, so I started to scan the room. A few rows ahead of me a middle-aged man ran on a treadmill. His back was to me, and all I could make out was a comb-over hairdo and a T-shirt advertising a termite removal company. For some reason, I was certain he was A) single, and B) extremely unattractive to me. Why are all the eligible men such dorks? I wondered. Then I quickly added, "cancel, cancel."

Before I knew it, I was surrounded on both sides by women of various ages who had also discovered the joys of recumbent bicycling. I'm going to be emotionally as well as physically healthy, I thought, recalling Denise's pep talk. Up in front of me and to the left, I noticed an elderly man lying on his side on a mat. For a brief second, I contemplated notifying the front desk that the man was in the midst of a stroke, but I didn't want to appear to be an alarmist. A few minutes later, he rolled onto his back, so at least I knew he was alive. I wouldn't even go to a gym if I was your age, I thought. I don't want strangers mopping me up off a floor.

I exercised on the bike for thirty minutes and couldn't find any single men on the gym floor. Feeling sweaty and disheveled, I headed toward the ladies' locker room. Halfway down the steps, I encountered a man with bulging biceps and sandy brown hair. The age seemed about right, so I smiled. In what seemed to be the supreme sacrifice, he smiled back. No decent single man is interested in me, I thought. Then quickly, "cancel, cancel."

When I got back to my office, I told the twenty-eight-year-old guy who sat behind me that I had been to the gym. I thought he would like that because I knew he worked out regularly. Dan was living with his girlfriend whom he would probably marry once she gave him an ultimatum that she would move out otherwise.

Why am I the only one who has to bear the cross of eternal loneliness?

I must have unknowingly muttered part of the thought out loud, because Dan asked me what I had said.

"Cancel, cancel," I told him.

Chapter 5

Cancel, Cancel Redux

Not long after Barbara, Dr. Gerrie and Denise were done with me, I was sitting in my cubicle at work fretting about all their advice when a book fell off my shelf and onto my head.

"God damn it!" I cursed.

Dan, the guy who sat behind me, jumped to his feet. "Wendy, are you okay?"

"No, I'm not okay!" I growled. "These things always happen to me. Why me?"

"Wendy, calm down," said Dan.

"Don't tell me what to do!" I sniped back. "I've had it with people telling me what to do!"

"Sorry," he said.

Suddenly filled with remorse, I apologized. "I've just been a little tense lately," I said.

Isabel had been pushing relaxation techniques like body scanning and deep breathing on me for a long time, but I had dismissed all of her suggestions with "I can't," to which she replied, "You can't or you won't?"

"I just can't relax without a Vicodin in my system," I had insisted.

"You can't solve all your problems with pills," Isabel had persisted.

"No, but I'm reasonably sure I can solve most of them that way," I had said. I'm so exhausting, I had thought.

"Anyone can train her mind," said Isabel. Clearly, we were at an impasse.

Flashback: I tell my mother that I want to go to a holistic doctor to work on the constipation I suffer from due to taking anti-depressants. "What?" she yells. "You're going to one of those quacks? Don't you know it's all a bunch of bullshit?"

My mother, who has two sons who are doctors, doesn't have anything nice to say about anyone who is not an M.D. I shelve my plans to go to a holistic healer.

Back to the present: Despite my mother's argument, I took Isabel's advice and started looking around for ways to relax—God knows I needed them after Barbara, Gerrie and Denise. I was skimming through a New Age magazine when I saw the ads for classes in aromatherapy and yoga, which promised to bring peace and contentment. I e-mailed my British literary agent and asked him which class he thought I should take. He and I were already in a codependent relationship in that he enabled me to believe fantasies that we could both get rich off my writing, and he was the one who had suggested that I attempt a book on depression to begin with.

"I would say the aromatherapy first," he e-mailed me. "That way, you will be a bit laid back and able to cope with the muscle spasms from yoga." Then he asked me, "Have you ever seen that yogic flying? Now that is something. It calls for everything from incredible concentration to intense bowel control. Please advise if you acquire the skill, and send me a video."

"I've never heard of yogic flying," I wrote back. "Is that like when the Dalai Lama gets shot out of a cannon?"

My agent wrote, "It works like this. You sit cross-legged on the floor, and by flexing your gluteus maximus (bum) you propel yourself several feet through the air and land some distance away."

"Are you serious?" I e-mailed.

"Yes," responded my agent. "Somehow the yoga lot think this confers peace and harmony or something like that. There is a political party in this country, and I bet you thought California was home to all the nuts, that advocates a large number of these flyers doing their thing near the houses of parliament and influencing the world."

I knew I wasn't quite up to yogic flying, so I decided to take my agent's advice and take the aromatherapy class first. I left a message for the teacher and got a message back from someone who was either borderline retarded or had a severe speech impediment. She told me that there was going to be a fair prior to the workshop, and that if I attended it, the instructor would give me a discount on the aromatherapy class.

A week later, I found myself at the Center for Personal Transformation.

"It's five dollars for an all-day pass to the lectures and demonstrations, but if you want a psychic reading, that will be twenty-five dollars for twenty minutes," a woman who looked like Anne Rice told me at the door.

I forked over the five bucks and told her that I would forgo the reading because I already had a psychic I depended on, whose predictions never came true.

I walked down a narrow hallway to a gift table that displayed spiritual books at fifty percent off, a variety of gemstones and a slew of silver jewelry.

"What would be a good stone for me?" a lady asked.

"The Dalmatian jasper," stated the woman behind the table. "If there's a hole in your aura field, it will connect with it and mend it."

"Mend it how?" asked the woman.

"It'll sew it right up," said the woman behind the table.

"Sew it. Really?" exclaimed the stone shopper.

"Definitely," said the woman behind the table.

At this point, three doddering old women from the Church of Faith entered and handed out flyers to everyone at the gift table. "We meet here on Sundays," one of the evangelicals said to me.

"I'll be sure to come," I said, fearful of inducing the wrath of God if I refused.

A man approached the lady behind the table.

"What are you looking for?" she asked as he randomly picked up various stones.

"I want to become more psychic," said the man.

"You have to put your mind down here," she told him, putting her hand on her belly.

"It feels warm," said the man following suit.

"It helps you see into other people's bodies," said the woman.

"Wow," said the man.

"Remember, your third eye is always open," the woman advised.

"I will remember that," said the man, plunking down a dollar for the stone.

I moved a little closer to the table and spotted a lavender stone labeled, "Push love into action."

"What is this for?" I asked the woman.

"That's rhodonite," said the woman. "If you're just hanging around waiting for things to happen on the romantic front, this will force action."

"I'll take one of those," I said eagerly, handing over a bill. It occurred to me that despite all the advice I had heard in the previous few months, I was still on the lookout for the magic solution to my problems. Then again, hadn't the other stone shoppers been searching for the same thing? Was I really so different?

I asked the rhodonite woman where I might find Jill, the aromatherapy instructor, so that I could prepay for her class.

"Jill's in the gift shop," said the woman. I trotted down the hall toward the gift shop. On the way, I encountered a high-strung looking thirty-something woman with a young daughter in tow. The young girl was crying.

"You have to be quiet now," the woman whispered to her.

"Why?" she demanded. "I want to go back to the gift shop."

"Mommy is getting a reading," said the young mother sharply.

"Like Harry Potter?" asked her daughter.

"Sort of," said the woman.

Thank God I don't have to expose a child to this, I thought. I had never wanted children because it took all the energy I had just to get out of bed in the morning, and I was reasonably sure I couldn't help another human being do it. On a deeper level, I did not want to bring another depressed person into this world, given the difficulties I had experienced getting through life. It did not seem fair.

When I got to the gift shop, I was confronted by a leggy platinum blonde in her fifties.

"Can I help you with something?" she asked me.

I recognized her voice as the one on my answering machine.

"I'm looking for Jill," I said. "I want to sign up for the aromatherapy class."

"Jill's at the table down the hall," drawled the woman.

"Is there even a Jill?" I muttered under my breath. I stopped to take a look at some of the books in the gift shop—titles like *Angels Versus Angel Food Cake* and *They Are My Dreams and You Can't Have Them*. I noticed a closed door leading to another room at the back of the shop. I could hear voices beyond it.

"What's in there?" I asked a woman standing next to me.

"That's where the chiropractor is giving demonstrations," she said.

"Oh," I said. "Do they really work?"

"I don't know," said the woman. "My sister needed relief from sinus pressure and she's been in there for over an hour."

Are you sure that's the only relief she needed? I wanted to ask, but restrained myself. I walked back out into the hallway to look for the elusive Jill. Minutes later, the chiropractor emerged from his exam room and spoke to another woman.

"I had spinal meningitis, but not the deadly kind," the woman said.

"You had an inflammation of your meninges," said the chiropractor. "That's what meningitis means."

"Are my meninges bad now?" the woman wanted to know.

"It depends on your spinal column," said the chiropractor, who then embarked on a long-winded explanation of why she needed his services. There certainly is no dearth of people wanting to take your money when you're in search of help, I thought.

I walked back down to the gift table and on the way bumped into a woman in her thirties who was so slight that she looked like she would fall over if you blew on her at the right angle. She had a Twiggy style hairdo and wore a black T-shirt and white capris.

"Are you Jill?" I asked her.

"Yes," she answered, smiling wanly.

"My name is Wendy," I said. "I'd like to sign up for the aromatherapy class on the nineteenth."

"Great," she said, leading me back to the leggy blonde in the gift shop. As I took her full measure, I decided that she had once been a Radio City Rockette who had most likely suffered a severe head injury. How she got to the Center for Personal Transformation was a mystery.

"It's thirty-five dollars if you leave a deposit today," Jill informed me.

"Okay," I said.

Back to the Rockette. "Sally, sign Wendy up for the aromatharapy class," Jill instructed.

Sally took out a piece of notebook paper and wrote down my name and phone number. "How much is the class?" she asked Jill.

"It's thirty-five dollars if she leaves a ten-dollar deposit today."

"Okay," said Sally. "And when is it?" she asked.

"It's the nineteenth," said Jill pleasantly.

"And how much is it?" inquired Sally.

"It's thirty-five dollars if she leaves a ten-dollar deposit today."

"Okay," said Sally. "And when is it?"

Now I was losing my patience. I had a very short fuse for other people because I had a short fuse for myself. I felt that I always had to get things right the first time, so why shouldn't everybody else? I often found myself angry over minor infractions like this, as all the rage I had felt as a child was still working its way out of my adult system.

"It's the nineteenth and its thirty-five dollars!" I interjected, my voice rising a decibel.

"Okay, all you had to do was tell me," snapped Sally. She then presented me with an appointment card for the aromatherapy class. I noticed that it was about time for the first lecture to begin, so I thanked Sally and Jill and trotted off to the classroom. At the front of the room was a fortyish man dressed in a cheap suit and possessing a nose that looked exactly like an eagle's beak.

"Are you here for the lecture on stress and anxiety?" he asked me.

"Yes," I said, noting that there was only one other person in a roomed filled with about thirty seats. She was a nondescript, heavy-set, middle-aged woman with short dirty blonde hair and glasses.

"Great," said our instructor. "I mean, it's not great that you suffer from anxiety, but it's great that you're doing something about it."

I smiled back cautiously. The lack of participation bothered me. Was I the only one on Long Island who suffered from stress and anxiety? Apparently, while everyone else was out doing fun things like sailing and bird watching, I was in a dark room with someone intent on capitalizing on my emotional problems.

"Now I'm going to distribute a handout," said the lecturer, who identified himself as Frank. "I want you to look at this anxiety symptom checklist and check off every item that applies to you. If you have more than three in each category, you have an anxiety problem."

I looked down at the checklist of physiological, cognitive and emotional responses and decided that virtually every item applied to me. When I looked up, Frank was staring at me.

"Can I ask you what your name is?" Frank inquired.

"I'm Wendy," I said reluctantly.

"Wendy, would you like to share what you checked off?"

Not exactly.

"Okay," I said.

In an instant, I decided I was going to reveal only two items per category. "Physiologically, I get butterflies in my stomach and I am fatigued. Cognitively, I get thoughts like, 'I can't do it' and 'What if I'm making a fool of myself?' Emotionally, I feel embarrassed and criticized."

"Good," said Frank. "Now we're getting somewhere." He moved on to the other lady in the room, who identified herself as a medical receptionist named Miriam. Miriam revealed that three of the symptoms in each category applied to her, including the response to "Get out of here" when she was confronted with a group of "negative" people.

"If you didn't leave, what would happen?" Frank asked her.

"I would get sleepy," said Miriam.

This seemed a highly unlikely response to a panic attack, but then I didn't know much about Miriam yet.

"To say you are having a 'panic attack' is inaccurate," Frank said. "Panic can't attack you. Have you ever seen panic on the street?"

Frank waited for Miriam and me to laugh, but we didn't, so he proceeded. "Anxiety is a manifestation of things suppressed in the past that are now coming out." He waited for his pearls of wisdom to settle in on us, but having been in therapy for years, this was simply not news to me. Frank, however, was not giving up. "When you have anxiety today, it is not about what's happening to you today. It's about what happened to you in the past."

Miriam nodded appreciatively, while I suppressed an eyeball roll.

"I have a theory called the dumpster theory," said Frank. "That's when everyone piles all this garbage into you and one day the dumpster becomes full and you can't accept any more garbage."

There were more appreciative nods from Miriam.

"Then you have to empty the dumpster," Frank continued. "And you can't do it alone."

As I wondered if Frank had any type of degree, high school or otherwise, Miriam asked, "What if you've been doing that and you still feel anxious?"

"Then there's still more junk in the dumpster," said Frank proudly.

"Well, I've been working on myself with a therapist for the past ten years and I still feel anxious," said Miriam.

Frank looked like a tiger poised to strike. "Well, if a child has a teacher for world history and he's teaching American history, then you have to look at the teacher because he's misdirecting the child," he said.

Miriam either could not or did not want to apply the analogy to her own situation. "I do feel a little better," she said.

"A little better? After ten years?" Frank asked.

"I've been in therapy for ten years, too," I interjected.

"And how do you feel?" asked Frank.

"A little better," I said.

At this point, Frank handed out brochures for his therapy business. "We only take six months to a year," said Frank. "We have a session, and if you have different issues, we refer you to specialists in those areas."

And how long would that go on? I wanted to ask. Until the next millennium?

"If you want, you can talk to a tree week after week and give the tree a hundred dollars," Frank said. "That's what it's like with certain therapists."

"I never went week after week," Miriam said in her therapist's defense.

"You have to get on the road to peace, happiness and contentment. It's a journey you take," Frank responded, totally ignoring Miriam's argument. "There are groups that say, 'Follow our path.' But you can't zigzag. You have to stay on your own path."

"That's true," said Miriam.

"I want to show you some things," said Frank, one by one withdrawing sheets of paper with sayings on them like "Stay in the moment," and "Change is constant. Welcome it." When he was through, he thanked us for coming, gave us the names of some books to read and told us that "ego" stands for "ease God out." I sat there wondering if he was working on commission for the doddering evangelicals that I had met earlier.

After Frank left, Miriam came over and sat next to me. "He doesn't know anything about my relationship with my therapist," she whispered urgently. "I only went to the man every six weeks and he counseled me through two divorces. We became friends."

"I'm on friendly terms with my therapist too," I said.

"I'm not going to Frank," said Miriam.

"Me neither," I said. "I don't like therapists who trash other therapists. It's not sporting."

"I know what you mean," said Miriam.

Then I thought, maybe Miriam and I were both guilty of emotional reasoning. In other words, we felt a certain way—anxious and depressed—so we believed that there was something terribly wrong with us.

"Look," I said to Miriam, "maybe we really aren't as bad off as we feel we are."

"There's an idea," said Miriam, blinking rapidly.

I thought about my experiences with Winning Ways, the self-esteem class and the relationship gurus. What had compelled me to seek them out was my feeling that I was deficient in some way, and they had confirmed this feeling. But maybe this feeling wasn't the truth. This feeling may have led me to think a certain way about myself that was actually inaccurate. Isabel liked to call these thoughts a cognitive distortion.

"Maybe," I said to Miriam, "even if we feel bad about ourselves, it doesn't mean that we are inherently flawed. Just because we feel flawed doesn't mean we are flawed."

"Yes," said Miriam, "but what do we do about it?"

"We have to reason with ourselves," I said, thinking of Denise's "cancel, cancel." "We have to counter all the negative thinking."

"That makes sense," said Miriam.

"I'm glad we had this chat," I said, patting Miriam's hand. "I'm determined to take action."

"Me, too," said Miriam.

"Let's throw Frank in the dumpster too," I concluded.

"I'm with you," said Miriam.

Walking down the hall a little later, I bumped into Jill coming from behind a closed door.

"Would you like a Reiki demonstration?" she asked me.

"What's that?" I responded.

"It's an ancient healing art used to balance and align your energy centers," she replied. "Do you want to try?"

In my heyday, I would have said "No," but Jill was so sincere, I couldn't turn her down. I followed her into a carpeted room with peach walls. On one side was a green and white striped couch with large green throw pillows. Across from that sat a brown recliner. Soothing music played in the background and lit candles filled the room.

"Where should I sit?" I wanted to know.

"Take off your jacket and sit in the recliner," Jill instructed me. She sat on the couch, opened a small vial filled with oil and rubbed it into her palms. "I'm a distributor," she told me. At first, I wasn't clear as to what she meant, but then I realized that Jill was trying to sell me oils. I smiled back in a non-committal way.

Jill got up and quietly walked behind me, resting her oily hands on the top of my head. Great, just what I needed. More oil at the roots of my hair. She held her hands there for several minutes as my eyes became locked on the flickering flame of a candle positioned directly in my line of vision. The smell of the oil, I must admit, was pleasing. The whole scene was sort of captivating.

After several more seconds, Jill moved one hand to my forehead and the other to the back of my head and held them there again. Slowly she worked her way down my neck to the top part of my chest. What if she touches one of my boobs? I thought. What if Reiki actually means *pervert* in Hindu? What will I do? Then I countered with: You'll be able to handle it if that happens. You can cope by telling her that you have to get up now. I felt a cough brewing in my throat but dared not let go of it lest it interfere with the energy flow. Then I felt an itch on my eyelid but was again afraid to do anything about it.

When she was finished stroking me on my upper body, without touching my boobs, Jill walked out from behind me and sat back down on the couch. "That was Reiki," she said.

"Oh?" I said.

"How do you feel?" she inquired.

"How am I supposed to feel?" I asked.

"Relaxed," Jill said.

"I do sort of feel relaxed," I said, not wanting to disappoint. And the truth was, I did feel somewhat relaxed. Jill was so serene, her very presence was calming. It was as though she had the key to happiness and was interested in sharing it with anyone who was capable of understanding it. I wasn't counting myself in that category yet, and clearly neither was Jill.

"Sometimes you don't feel relaxed until several days later," Jill said.

"So you mean that someone will cut me off in traffic and suddenly I'll feel relaxed?" I asked.

Jill smiled, but I wasn't sure that she got the joke.

"Those oils smelled really good," I continued. "What were they?"

"Lavender and sandalwood," said Jill.

"Do they help with insomnia?" I asked. "I have trouble falling and staying asleep."

"They are great for that," said Jill. "And you need to stay away from peppermint and lemon. Those scents wake you up."

"Peppermint and lemon," I wrote in my notebook.

"You'll learn all about that in the aromatherapy class," noted Jill.

I held out my hand and got an extremely limp, fleeting handshake back.

"Thanks," I said. "I'm going to listen to some more lectures." I walked back down the hall to the classroom and saw Miriam walking out. "What was this seminar?" I asked.

"Women's spirituality," she reported.

"Was it any good?" I asked.

"Not really. It's just a group of women who sit around bitching about men every Wednesday," Miriam replied.

"I have to bitch about men more than one day of the week," I said.

Miriam giggled. "That was funny," she said.

Maybe some people do get my sense of humor, I thought. "Are you staying for the 'Benefits of Yoga' lecture?" I asked Miriam.

"Yes, I want to hear about that," she said. "I've taken three yoga classes."

"How were they?" I wanted to know.

"The first one was really good, but after that it got a little hairy," she said.

"Hairy? Like what?" I inquired.

"You know. You had to hang upside down and all," she answered.

"Hang upside down?" I murmured, thinking about the friend who had hesitantly agreed to take a yoga class with me. Again, Miriam and I were the only two people in the seminar room waiting for a lecture. About fifteen minutes into our wait, we learned that the yoga instructor was "running late." Fifteen minutes later, she still had not arrived.

"Do you think this means that there are no benefits to doing yoga?" I asked Miriam.

"No, there are," she insisted quite seriously. Clearly my sense of humor goes only so far with Miriam, I thought.

At the top of the hour, a woman dressed all in white, from her lab coat down to her technician's shoes, entered the classroom and told us that Benefits of Yoga had been cancelled and that she was an aesthetician and healer who was going to give a talk about increasing our energy. Miriam and I smiled pleasantly.

The woman began her talk by saying, "There are seven openings in the body where energy flows in and out."

This was curious to me because I could count only three, maybe four, bodily orifices tops, but I decided not to make an issue of it. The woman proceeded to list the seven places, calling them "chakras."

"By recognizing your energy sources, you increase your awareness and can move into higher realms of thought," she said.

Again I was skeptical. But then I thought: If I don't let anybody here in, Jill won't give me the key to happiness.

At this point, a morbidly obese man or woman (I couldn't tell which) entered the classroom with two skinny people in tow.

"We were just talking about energy flow," said the healer.

"Is there any place to get a meal around here?" said the morbidly obese person. This led to a discussion of the neighborhood eating establishments that Miriam, who lived nearby, was more than happy to take part in. At the end of the discussion, the three latecomers picked up and left.

The healer went back to her discourse on the connection between the mental and physical body and said we should be kind to our energy centers by taking hot baths with Epsom salts, ginger root and rose petals. This would soften our muscles and allow us to listen to our inner voice, thereby expanding our consciousness to a higher level.

That'll never work for me, I thought. But then I countered with, Why not at least give it a try before you condemn it?

At this juncture, an elderly Jewish couple, who most likely thought the Center for Personal Transformation was serving early bird dinner specials, entered the room.

"I have pain in my shoulder blades," Miriam piped up before the couple could say anything. "What does that mean?"

"That means you have a wounded heart," said the healer.

"Oh," murmured Miriam.

"Now, to get your chakras back into balance, I suggest you take hundreds of rose petals and lay down on them, so you are blanketed by love. Then take emerald crystals and place them on your back."

"Oh, really?" said Miriam. "That's an interesting solution."

I'll say.

Suddenly, the elderly man jumped into the conversation. "Have you ever heard of moldite?" he asked the healer.

"Is that a beige stone?" she asked him.

"No, it's green. It's like a meteorite," he answered.

"From outer space?" asked the healer.

"Yes," said the man.

"Well, I would rub some sage in that so there's no strange energy coming through," she said.

"I have a fear of doctors and medicine," said the older gentleman. "What could you do for that?"

"Probably guided meditation," said the healer.

"You don't do regression hypnosis?" asked the man, clearly trying to show his metaphysical prowess.

"I only do that for smoking," said the healer.

The elderly gentleman went on questioning the healer for several minutes, and when she could no longer take it, she thanked us all and made a quick escape. Meanwhile, the elderly gentleman walked over to Miriam and complimented her on the gemstone she was wearing around her neck. I realized that this was the moment I had been waiting for to escape everyone from the Center for Personal Transformation.

"I'm going to go," I whispered to Miriam after the older man had left.

"Take care," she said to me.

"You too," I said, shaking her hand. I almost wanted to get her phone number so we could stay in touch and struggle together, but I didn't have the nerve to ask for it. Still, just knowing that there was someone else out there who felt like she was still not "cured" after years of therapy made me feel as though I wasn't so unusual after all. Maybe it was a process and Miriam and I were making progress in such small increments that we didn't even recognize it.

When I got home, I could still smell the Reiki oils on my hair. Oddly, it did at first make me feel very relaxed. Maybe there is something to this, I thought. Then I ate some leftover Thai food and got an attack of diarrhea.

Several weeks later, I was in my friend Marie's apartment trying to get her three cats to come out from under her bed. Afterwards, I noticed a newsletter from a veterinary practice on her kitchen table. On the front cover was an article about a cat whose cancer had gone into remission with holistic treatment.

"Do you believe in holistic medicine for people?" I asked her.

"I think there's something to it or you wouldn't hear all these success stories," she said.

And she was right. Why not try to keep an open mind, I thought? Just because my mother was narrow-minded didn't mean I had to be. In fact, I was almost coming to believe that I should do the opposite of whatever my mother said. So I decided to go back to the Center for Personal Transformation to take the aromatherapy class.

When I got there a couple of weeks later and Jill saw me, her whole face lit up.

She sincerely wants to help, I thought.

Jill led me into a room with mauve-colored walls and a large, comfortable looking beige couch. A wood coffee table held a bunch of vials and several handouts.

"I'm not sure if anyone else is coming," Jill said. "There's another woman, but ..."

"That's okay," I said.

Everyone but me is already relaxed. They don't need to take this class, I thought. Then I countered with the question: What evidence do I have that everyone else is relaxed? Absolutely none. In fact, my friend Marie, a non-neurotic, had signed up for yoga with me because she wanted to learn how to relax.

"So you don't have a problem with being the only student?" Jill asked.

Should I? I wanted to ask. I was afraid to offend Jill just in case she was my savior.

"We have green bottles today," said Jill, gesturing toward the table. I guess I must have looked very unimpressed because Jill immediately added, "It's very hard to get green bottles."

"Great," I said, trying to muster as much enthusiasm as I could.

Jill sat down next to me on the couch and opened a loose-leaf binder that she had placed in her lap. "Do you know anything about aromatherapy?" asked Jill hopefully.

"Not really," I said.

At first Jill looked disappointed, but she regrouped sufficiently to read the following explanation from the pages in her binder. "Aromatherapy can be defined as the art and science of utilizing naturally extracted aromatic essences from plants to balance, harmonize and promote the health of body, mind and spirit. Aromatherapy is both a preventative approach as well as an active treatment during acute and chronic stages of illness and disease."

"How is it supposed to do that?" I asked tentatively.

"Well," responded Jill, "it has to do with your chakras."

"Chakras?" I asked.

"You know what they are, right?" Jill inquired.

"I forget," I said softly.

Jill looked severely dismayed.

What if she gives me a failing grade, just like Barbara from Winning Ways and Dr. Gerrie from the self-esteem class? Then I countered with: There is no reason I can't do well at this. I am not going to catastrophize.

Jill picked up a handout from the coffee table and gave it to me. I looked down and saw a drawing of what appeared to be a naked man sitting in the lotus position. My eye was immediately drawn to the area where the man's penis would be. It was labeled the "sacral chakra" for life force, strength, power and vitality. I thought that any man would be hard pressed to contradict that statement.

"These are all your chakras," Jill said. "In other words, they are the energy centers of your soul. Sometimes the chakras become unbalanced and we have to balance them again."

"Of course we have to do that," I said. Jill did not laugh.

"Are there any chakras you're having difficulty with?" Jill asked.

I looked back at the sheet and saw that the sacral chakra also included creativity, self-confidence and well being. "My sacral chakra," I murmured. "What's good for that?"

Jill gave me another handout. I glanced at it and saw another drawing of a naked man. This one, however, had circles of different colors going from the top of the head to the groin area.

"You're talking about the second chakra," said Jill. "You can see the recommended oils."

I looked more closely and saw an oil called ylang-ylang, which was supposed to release sexuality blocks.

"My main problem is with insomnia," I said, although my inability to relax during sex did prey on my mind. Why couldn't I just have been born a wild woman? I thought. Then I countered the negative with: How many wild women have you actually met?

"I remember the last time we met you told me about lavender and sandalwood for insomnia," I said to Jill.

"Yes," she said. "I just put three drops of lavender in bath water and I am out."

"In the bath?" I asked.

Jill laughed. "No, when I get to bed," she said.

Maybe Jill does appreciate my sense of humor somewhat.

"Lavender is also good for burns, cuts, scrapes and muscle pain," Jill continued. "In fact, its use can be traced back to the origins of modern aromatherapy."

I tried to look interested and apparently succeeded, because Jill then told me that in 1928 a French chemist named Gattefosee dunked his hand in lavender after sustaining burns in a laboratory explosion and realized its power to heal.

I wondered what a chemist was doing with a vat of lavender oil to begin with, but Jill babbled on that aromatherapy could even be traced back to Biblical times, when frankincense and myrrh were rubbed on Christ's feet when he was a baby. I must have appeared absorbed in this tidbit of trivia because Jill went on to enthuse about the fact that Cleopatra burned opium oil as a way to keep Marc Antony interested in her and that the Indians, Japanese and Chinese subsequently used therapeutic oils in their daily lives. "The Eastern world is much more advanced than we are," Jill maintained. "Did you know that every school child in the East is taught Reiki?"

What the hell for? I wanted to joke. Then I wondered if depression was as rampant in the East as it was in the Western world. It seemed to me that the Western world was so achievement-oriented that it probably made depressives living here feel more ashamed about our inability to keep up than, say, those living in Buddhist countries such as Thailand and Cambodia. Depressives could probably learn a lot from the East, I concluded.

"Now I want you to take a sniff of each of the oils I have here and tell me what the smell feels like," Jill said.

"I'll try," I said.

I don't know what my feelings are, much less what my feelings smell like, I thought. Then I countered with: You can try and identify your feelings. You're better at that now than you were before you started with Isabel.

"Okay, here's the lavender," said Jill, handing me a small vial.

"I feel relaxation," I said, after taking a whiff.

"Relaxation?" said Jill.

"Yes, but that isn't an emotion, is it?" I said.

"Well …" said Jill, who was such a nurturing individual that she did not want to hurt my feelings. "Here's the lemon," she said, offering me another bottle.

I smelled the lemon. "It makes me feel alert," I said.

"Yes, lemon is great for that," Jill rejoined, "but you have to be careful of the citrus oils because you can get an allergic reaction if they get mixed with any type of household cleaners."

I was having a vision of telling an EMT that I was having a lemon oil emergency when Jill picked up a vial of peppermint and handed it to me. "Now this should wake you up, but it's also good for headaches, morning sickness and a sore throat."

But can it do anything for anthrax attacks? I wanted to ask, but again decided against it. Jill had been gracious enough to laugh at one of my jokes and I didn't want to get greedy. Thankfully, she had decided not to ask me about my feelings anymore and just passed the remaining bottles—eucalyptus, orange and tea tree—along for me to sniff.

"Now, let's make some patches," Jill said after I was done.

Can we make a nicotine patch? I wanted to ask.

"You said you were interested in the lavender, so we'll start with that," Jill said. She opened a package containing a piece of gauze and had me pour a few drops of lavender oil on it.

"Fold the gauze and put it in a plastic bag," instructed Jill. I did as I was told. "Now keep that in your pocketbook and take a sniff every time you feel your energy centers are unbalanced."

I began to envision opening my bag to take out my wallet and having the cafeteria workers and several employees wondering out loud where that pungent smell was coming from. No, I determined, this would not go over well amongst non-believers.

"You can also use a clay pot that you hang around your neck," said Jill, showing me an example. Again, I pictured co-workers at the copy machine asking me where I got such an unusual piece of jewelry. "It's for my chakras," would definitely provide them with more gossip for the office rumor mill. Apparently, the circles that Jill moved in did not think wearing a clay pot around your neck was strange. A part of me wanted to move in those circles, too.

Lost in my thoughts, I hardly heard Jill tell me that she was going to lead me in a few minutes of meditation.

"Meditation?" I squeaked. (After all, I had signed on only for aromatherapy.)

"Have you ever meditated?" Jill wanted to know.

"I can't," I said. "My mind wanders."

"Every time you have a thought just picture it in a bubble, and let the bubble float away," she said.

Since this had never occurred to me, I decided that I would try to give it a whirl. Jill had me sit back in the couch with my legs uncrossed, my palms outstretched, and my thumbs and third fingers touching. She turned on some soothing music and told me to picture myself sitting in a crystalline pyramid bathed in a golden glow. This was all I needed to hear to tune her out and to start obsessing about a hemorrhoid condition I had recently developed. As much as I tried to visualize my hemorrhoids in a bubble, I could not. My mind, as always, became a cauldron of competing thoughts. And there was no way out. I'm bad, I thought. I can't even meditate right. Then I thought: Don't be so hard on yourself. It's difficult to meditate and it takes practice.

"How was that?" asked Jill when she finally finished her monologue.

"It's kind of difficult for me," I said, not wanting to let her down.

"It's hard at the beginning, but you can train your mind," she responded

"I'll try," I volunteered.

"If you're interested, we have a meditation group that meets every Thursday night," she offered.

"I'll think about it," I said.

If I couldn't meditate this time, I'll never be able to meditate, I thought. Then I countered with: If I practice, the odds are that I will be capable of meditating,

"Okay," said Jill. "If you're interested, just contact me."

"Yes, I will," I said.

"Now before you go I want to give you a Reiki and aromatherapy treatment." She ushered me over to a huge wicker chair with a soft fabric cushion. I sat down and closed my eyes. Jill stood behind me and started touching me the way she had done in the Reiki session I had had previously. She put a gauze pad bathed in lavender in front of my nose. I started to feel somewhat tranquil when she came in front of me, told me she had to balance my emotional centers and placed one hand on my boobs and the other on my stomach. I didn't know whether I should scream for help or offer thanks for the therapeutic treatment. I decided to do neither.

༆

When I awoke the next morning my forehead and right eyelid were painful and swollen. I was sure it was an allergic reaction to the aromatherapy oils. I went to the office, where a co-worker asked if I was the victim of domestic abuse. The next day my eye turned completely black and blue. Now I was certain that Jill had unleashed some sort of spiritual hex on me. "That aromatherapy freak jinxed me," I told my friend Joan.

"No, she didn't," Joan insisted. "You probably punched yourself in the eye."

"I think I did something to my eye in the middle of the night," I told Dr. Parise the next day.

"Well, that's highly likely," he said. "Sleepwalking is one of the most common side effects of the sleeping pill I prescribed for you. You're in such a deep sleep, you have no recollection of what you've done in the middle of the night. You could have walked into a wall."

"Really?" I said.

Dr. Parise nodded. "The classic example is when a man on sleeping pills gets up in the middle of the night and pees in his closet without ever realizing it."

"That is not good," I said.

"It's time for you to get off the sleeping pills," said my doctor.

I was almost ready to consider yogic flying.

Chapter 6

Weighty Issues

Although my eye healed in about a week, the near-fatal sleepwalking incident got me to thinking about my physical health and wellbeing. After a break of several weeks, I had once again resumed exercise on my recumbent bike, yet my weight had barely decreased at all. I knew that part of this had to do with the fact that the anti-depressant that I was on, Elavil, left me feeling hungry most of the time. When I asked Dr. Parise about switching to one of the newer medications, he told me that I needed a sedating anti-depressant and that all of the medications in this class increased appetite.

To make matters worse, I had also heard a report on the radio that said it was harder for depressed people to lose weight than for the general population. This had depressed me even further. Wasn't there anything depressed people had an easier time with than well-adjusted people? Why was everything such a struggle? Then I countered with: If it's that difficult, give yourself extra credit for trying.

Then one day I went to a department store with my eternally thin mother and asked her to sit in the dressing room while I got some garments. This way, I figured, she would not know what size I was. When I came back with some tops and blazers in hand, my mother immediately told me that the items wouldn't cover my ass.

"So?" I said, wounded.

My mother pursed her lips. "I never thought you would have a problem with your weight," she said, shaking her head. A tear almost formed in my eye.

When I got home, I immediately went online and searched for weight loss help. I found a company called Maximum Health Inc., which boasted a 95 percent weight loss success rate and offered a complimentary consultation. "Complimentary" was the key word.

"Hiya, Wendy," said Ellen, when I called the company's New Mexico phone number.

"Hiya," I said back, hearing shades of Denise.

"What can I do for you, Wendy?" asked Ellen.

"Well, do you do what you do by phone?" I asked tentatively.

"To what exactly are you referring?" Ellen trilled.

This is not a good sign. "The weight loss plan," I explained.

"Yes, I do work with phone consultations because so much of our population goes north during the summer."

"Can I get my free consultation?" I whispered urgently.

I thought I heard Ellen yawn. Then she said, "How much do you need to lose?"

"About twenty pounds," I said.

"And how long have you had this excess weight?" she asked.

"Five years," I said.

"And how old are you?" Ellen inquired.

"Fortyish," I said.

"Gee," drawled Ellen. "You sound like you're twenty-three years old!"

"Thank you," I said, although I was unsure if this was a compliment. I had always looked and sounded a great deal younger than my age, which had consistently given me leverage when pitching my helplessness.

Ellen went on to tell me that I needed to get something called a body fat analysis and report the results to her. Then she would design a diet and exercise plan especially for me. Of course, she explained, the only way to get a body fat analysis was to obtain a piece of equipment that I could order online for a cost of eighty dollars.

"You need to get one that measures body fat in .01 increments," Ellen told me. "We need to get a reading on your lean body mass."

"Okay," I agreed. "Then what do your consultations cost?"

"You know," said Ellen, "I wish I could do this for free, I love it so much. But there is a fee of sixty dollars for each consultation."

"That's reasonable," I said. (At least she was willing to quote me a price, unlike that queen bitch at the video dating service.) At the close of our conversation, Ellen told me she was sending me a free weight loss CD. "Good luck, hon," she offered.

When I went online that evening to find the body fat analyzer that Ellen had recommended, I found out that not only did it cost $135, but it looked as difficult to operate as the International Space Station.

You'll never be able to use this thing, I thought. Then I countered with: You can always get a friend to help you out with it.

However, I decided to search for a less costly and less complicated method of losing weight and found an established online dieting site that an acquaintance had recommended. "It really works," she had told me, stuffing a Häagen Dazs ice cream down her throat. "It's all diet and exercise. No pills or shakes."

I went to the site, where I was invited to get a free profile. The first thing it asked was my age, weight, height and gender. Then, "What word best describes how you feel about your weight?" Since "shitty" was not a choice, I chose "frustrated," though I wished the other words—"negative," "angry" and "embarrassed"—were admissible as well.

Then I countered with: If you work hard, you can get back to feeling good about your body.

The fact was, I had been a size six up until the time I turned thirty-five, when my genes and anti-depressant took over and I mushroomed to a twelve. At forty years old, I was still a twelve and heavier than my sickly brother. My mother, of course, had pointed this out, which made me feel even more ashamed of my body. Now I decided that the next time I felt bad about being heavier than my brother, I would counter with the thought that it was perfectly natural for a healthy person to weigh more than a sickly person.

The Web site profile asked for my program goals. I marked the circle that indicated that I wanted to lose between ten and twenty pounds because even in the privacy of my own computer, I couldn't admit that I really wanted to lose about thirty pounds.

Next I was asked if I had certain health conditions such as diabetes and heart disease. I didn't have any of the diseases mentioned and was looking for a place for write-in illnesses when I came upon a behavioral analysis form. This asked me to agree or disagree with statements such as, "I have no doubt that I will reach my goal weight" and "While exercising I am focused on the task at hand and I enjoy myself." My first inclination was to disagree with all the positive statements, but I forced myself to be more sanguine.

After I selected a meal plan (low fat, low cholesterol, low sugar, and low threshold for pain), the words "Congratulations, Wendy" appeared on my computer screen. "Here is your weight loss plan." I noticed all sorts of colorful charts and graphs that revealed where I currently was in my weight loss journey (at the beginning) and where I needed to go (it was far). Then a page popped up that said, "Here's the deal. Thousands of women have found a fast and easy way to shed pounds. We offer you a customized weight loss program including a personalized shopping list, weekly meal plans and online emotional support around the clock."

I'm still not sure I can do this, I thought. Then, I countered with: If you put your mind to it, you can do it.

The page went on to tell me that if I followed the program, with the help of online peers, health experts and mentors, I could lose 1.8 pounds a week and keep it off. This was all I needed to see to sign up for a nine-week trial for forty-five dollars and order a four-cassette audio program from someone called a certified emotional support coach for another forty-five dollars. (Had he taken classes in fear, sadness and joy?) Following this, I was deposited at the Welcome Desk, where I noticed such posts from fellow e-dieters as, "I'm lazy and I need help," "I have to lose 30 pounds in a week," and "I'm 20 and I feel like 40."

I contemplated leaving my own post—something along the lines of "I have had my stomach stapled, but I still can't fit through my front door," but decided against it. It was too chancy to risk telling a joke to a bunch of strangers who might take me seriously.

The first two messages at my Welcome Desk were from Jennifer, my personal nutrition counselor. Jennifer gave me a long list of daily, weekly and monthly tasks I had to accomplish to lose the weight. It occurred to me that if I followed all of her prescriptions, I would never again have the time to take a leisurely shit. I thought about bringing this point up to Jennifer but didn't, for fear that she would share it with the rest of our little weight loss community.

When I checked out my personalized menu for the first week, I really began to worry. Here were instructions such as "take 1/2 teaspoon of cottage cheese, 1 cup of oatmeal, 3/4 of a teaspoon of honey, 3 1/2 strawberries, 1 blueberry and 1/2 of a Tic Tac." Who had the time to take all these measurements when running out the door to not be late for work? Furthermore, I spent eight hours a day at my job staring vacantly at a computer screen and had no desire to do it for an additional three hours when I got home at night.

I told myself that I had made a big weight loss mistake. I'm such an idiot, I thought. Then I countered with: Everybody makes mistakes. Just pretend you bought a pair of shoes that didn't fit right and you lost the receipt.

When I walked through my mother's door for dinner later that night, I quickly confessed my error.

"Can't you get your money back?" my mother predictably screeched.

"I'm not going to get my money back," I yelled. "Do you know how hard it is to get money back from these self-help people? They cling to you like balloons with static."

In truth, I was getting a little weary of all the self-help gurus I had met over the past few months. I felt that when a person needed help, as I did, she was an easy target for all sorts of charlatans. I decided that I needed to be a lot more careful about whom I trusted.

"You need to go back to Weight Watchers!" my mother screamed back.

"But I hated getting weighed in every week," I said.

Then I countered with: Why am I trying to make a positive thing negative?

"You lost weight when you did that!" my mother reminded me.

My mother got no argument. She was right (for once). I had lost ten pounds with Weight Watchers. I don't know whether it was the fear of a stranger recording my weight on a weekly basis or my admiration for the disgraced member of the British royal family who was WW's American spokesperson, but it was definitely time to go back.

"I'm going back to WW," I wrote my British agent. "You know that it's endorsed here by your Duchess of York."

"You mean the Duchess of Pork?" he e-mailed me. "She's not well liked here."

I made a notation that If I ever got to meet Sarah Ferguson, I would ask her if she had plans to go back to Britain to rehabilitate her image.

I planned to attend my first meeting that Saturday. Subsequently, I checked out WW's Internet site and decided to register there because it was free of charge. Instantly, a whole universe of message boards appeared before my eyes. I decided to lurk around the newbies board and found the following message: "I just started the program an hour ago and so far things are going good."

I took self-quizzes on the site and found that in addition to having an unhealthy body mass index of thirty, I suffered from something called stray food syndrome. (Like a raccoon, I ate all the food I could scavenge.)

The next night I received by mail a package from Maximum Health Inc. It included a small handwritten note from Ellen telling me that with her program I could lose thirty pounds in fifteen weeks, an orange refrigerator magnet in the shape of a foot and a CD entitled *Stop Dieting Forever: Lose Weight Permanently Without Taking Drugs*. I figured it couldn't hurt to listen so I popped the disc into my CD player and sat back. After some peppy upbeat music, a very authoritative male voice said, "Ellen, my mind is absolutely boggled by your success statistics regarding weight loss. How do you do it?"

"It's funny you should ask that," chirped Ellen. "We do it by providing training, coaching and counseling to our clients and by showing them how to have fun losing weight."

"Fun losing weight?" said the man, trying to sound as astounded as he possibly could. "How is that possible?"

"I'll tell you," said Ellen. "First of all, most diets are so complicated, they are simply too difficult for anyone to follow. There is even a diet where you are required to convert food amounts into a complex point system."

"Really?" gasped the man.

"Yes, really," said Ellen.

Now I started worrying. I knew that Ellen was implicitly criticizing the Weight Watchers program, which relied, in part, on a point system. Although I had decided to go with Weight Watchers again, it wouldn't take much to shake my confidence in this decision. I was always second-guessing myself and driving others to distraction with my incessant questions about whether they thought my choices were right or wrong. Often, all it took was one person stridently disagreeing with me to make me change my mind.

"Some diets you have to be a mathematician to use correctly," Ellen went on.

Just a minute, I felt like saying.

"And with some diets there's no follow-up support," Ellen continued. "They just weigh you in, give you a pat on the back and send you on your way."

I was getting terribly uneasy. I remembered that some of the WW "scale ladies" did get kind of cold and impersonal when they discovered that you had actually gained six ounces in a week rather than lost them. Sure, the lecturers told us that it was all about the process and not the outcome, but who could continuously endure the harsh looks of the scale ladies when you gained?

Now Ellen made veiled references to the Weight Watchers lecturers themselves. "Some programs don't even have trained health-care professionals to guide you through the program. They have administrators," she said with mild contempt.

With this point, I made a mental note to ask my WW lecturer about her background. Ellen finished her CD by offering testimonials from people who had used her program and doctors who had referred patients to it. "I realized that I don't have to be old and fat," one woman said. I wanted to ask her if Ellen's weight loss program had actually made her younger, but of course, there was no opportunity.

Despite the negative press, I showed up at one of the WW storefront offices the following Saturday afternoon. Nothing much had changed since I had last been there, except there were now closed venetian blinds in the windows, most likely to hide us disgraced fatties from the public. I walked over to a thirty-something woman behind the counter and said I wanted to join.

"Have you been here before?" she warbled.

"Yes," I whispered. "About a year ago."

Don't tell anyone I'm here, I thought. Then I countered with: There are plenty of other people here and you have nothing to be ashamed of.

"So you know how it works?" she asked.

"Yes," I said as firmly as possible. After I had filled out some forms, I went back to the woman at the front of the room. Now I noticed another woman behind the counter. She seemed to be in her fifties and wore her long black hair pulled back in a clip. In addition to being thin, she appeared to be the recipient of both a face-lift and a nose job. I was about to feel intimidated by her the way I had felt with Barbara from Winning Ways, but then I thought: why should I? Barbara had confessed that she had problems. Maybe this woman does too.

"You can step on the scale when you're ready," said the younger woman. I took off my sneakers and did as I was told. Since your weight only registered at a station behind the counter, I had to wait until she had filled out what would be my weekly progress report. The news was pretty dismal. You're fat. You'll always be fat,

I thought. Then I countered with: There's no reason you can't lose weight again.

I took a bunch of other materials the woman had to offer and stood off to the side, admiring the various WW products that were available for purchase.

"I don't even feel like I'm part of my family anymore," I overheard the thirty-something say.

"Honey, you have to structure your schedule," the plastic surgery veteran rejoined. Suddenly, I realized that she was the facilitator for the 1 p.m. meeting. I also realized that I did not have the nerve to ask her if she had a nutrition degree of some sort, so I walked into the meeting room and took a seat in the back row. Two easels supporting large tablets with blown up images of nutrition labels found on food packages stood at the front of the room before the blackboard.

Presently, an unfriendly woman in a khaki outfit with blood red polish on her finger and toenails entered the room and sat a few seats away from me in the back row. Following that, two young women in their twenties entered and sat on the other side of me. They did not appear to be overweight. Perhaps, I thought, they were guilty of emotional reasoning—they felt fat, so they thought they were fat. At least Miriam from the Center for Personal Transformation and I weren't the only ones guilty of distorted thinking.

Soon, the older woman entered the room and introduced herself as Margo.

"I lost sixty-five pounds ten years ago," she said. "And I've successfully kept it off through the Weight Watchers program."

We stared at her impassively. A few minutes later, three rail-thin Asian women who must have thought this was an origami class entered the room. I'll never be as thin as they, I thought. Then I countered with: Why would you want to be as thin as they?

Margot told us that today's lecture was going to be on the eight steps to healthy weight loss. "First, how was it at the scales?" she asked.

"I lost 1.5 pounds. I couldn't believe it," said the khaki woman.

"Did you go to that party?" Margo asked.

"Yes, but I watched my portions," said the khaki woman.

I never watch my portions, I thought, but then I thought: That's not true. You watched your portion size at your mother's the other night.

"That is fantastic!" Margo enthused to the khaki woman.

"I'm in a new weight range," pronounced the khaki woman.

"What's it been total now?" asked Margo.

"Twenty-five pounds," said the woman.

I'll never be able to lose twenty-five pounds, I thought. Then, on the other hand, I can make a stab at it.

Margo applauded the woman. "I think you are going to get a magnet today!" she proclaimed.

"Really?" trilled the woman.

"Most definitely," said Margo. "So today's class will just be a review for you."

The khaki woman evinced an air of superiority that was palpable. What makes you so great? I thought.

"Now," said Margo. "Is it true that with this program all you have to do is count your points?"

"Incorrect," said one of the Asians.

"Exactly," said Margo.

"You have to change the way you think about eating," said the khaki woman.

"Yes, and we have to pay attention to serving size," said Margo. "I want everyone to turn to page ten in their starter book."

We all did so.

"Can anyone tell me what it says?" asked Margo.

I decided that I didn't want to participate in this part of Margo's class, but it wasn't because I was afraid, like I had been at the self-esteem class with Dr. Gerrie. It was more because her questions were so easy to answer, I thought I'd let an academically challenged individual handle them.

"That page in the starter book says, 'Pay attention to serving sizes,'"said the khaki woman dutifully, making her bid to remain the teacher's pet.

If she wants to be teacher's pet that badly, let her, I thought. It's no reflection on me.

"Did you know that all of the weight gain we are experiencing in this country can be traced back to this epidemic of super-sizing?" said Margo. "The original McDonald's meal was 550 calories. Now it's over 1,500 calories."

The khaki woman gasped.

"Now, turn to page twelve," Margo resumed. "What does it say?"

"It says, 'Choose at least five servings of fruit and vegetables per day,'" said one of the Asians before the khaki woman could speak.

"Does anyone have a problem with this?" asked Margo. No one said anything. "Does anyone have any suggestions for getting more fruits and vegetables into their daily diets?" Again there was silence. Margo looked around the room for someone to participate.

"I bring fruits and vegetables to work in Baggies, and I eat them as snacks," I said when I could bear the silence no longer.

You participated! Yipee! I thought.

"That is fantastic," said Margo. "Anybody else?"

"I use the George Foreman grill," said the khaki woman. "And I juice."

"Everyone should juice," said Margo. I looked around the room and saw that most of my classmates were averting Margo's gaze. So I'm not the only one who doesn't juice, I thought.

"What else does page twelve say?" asked Margo. By this time I had decided that Margo was a lousy teacher, but that I couldn't let her sink.

"It says, 'choose at least two servings of milk and milk products a day,'" said the khaki woman, before one of the Asians could speak.

"Does anyone know what is in milk that we need?" asked Margo.

"Calcium," I answered, putting my bid in to be teacher's pet.

"That is correct," said Margo. "That can be milk, a smoothie or even a yogurt."

"I heard that the non-fat yogurts are worse than the low-fat yogurts because they have a lot of sugar in them," I chimed in.

"You are so right," said Margo. "Do you know that I don't have any 'diet' products in my house? People think they are going to lose weight by buying SnackWells or Entenmanns Light. Ridiculous."

We proceeded to go through the rest of the eight points, and when we were done, Margo asked if we had any questions or comments. Again there were none forthcoming.

"Is everyone keeping their daily journals?" Margo asked.

"I have them all here," said the khaki woman, reaching into her bag and withdrawing fifty loose pages clipped together.

"Why don't you just buy our personal diary?" pitched Margo. "That way you can condense."

"I'm obsessive," responded the khaki woman. "If I start something a certain way, I have to keep with it. I can't stop myself."

So I'm not the only person who can turn obsessive, I thought.

"You don't want to be all-or-nothing," Margo said.

"But I'm also goal oriented," explained the khaki woman.

"And that is a good thing," said Margo, intent on giving us positive messages.

"Do any of the new people have questions?" asked Margo. We stared back blankly. "This program is easy to understand, but difficult to do," she clucked.

"But it's worth it," said the khaki woman.

"I'll say," Margo responded. "Did you know that by the year 2020, one hundred percent of our population will be overweight and that by the year 2080, one hundred percent will be morbidly obese?"

At least I'll be dead by then, I thought. And then I countered with: but I'll be in a better place.

On Monday I received an e-mail from WW that told me a woman named Diane had lost seventy-two pounds with the program and had celebrated by getting a tattoo of Little Orphan Annie on her butt. I wondered what I would do if I lost thirty pounds. I thought that the first thing I would do was purchase new underwear, as Dr. Gerrie had noted that this was a prerequisite for high self-esteem.

As the day progressed, things did not go well. By the time lunch approached, I had already eaten ten points worth of food. I bought a turkey sandwich in the cafeteria, promptly threw out the bread and scarfed the turkey breast down like a hungry wolf. I decided that at dinner I would limit myself to a small can of vegetarian beans (two points), a nutrition bar (two points) and a sugar-free lime Jell-O (zero points), thereby barely staying within my daily allotment of points.

For a brief moment I considered the alternative Weight Watchers program called Core, in which you could eat as much as you want of some very specific things and only count points for the remainder. But when I looked up which items were a part of the Core program, I found that basically the only things you could eat without counting points were baking soda and cardboard. I didn't think it was for me.

When I got home that night I found my four-tape set from the online dieting program I had impulsively joined. I popped the first program, *The Psychology of Decision Making*, into the tape recorder. After some up-tempo music, another authoritative man told me he was going to awaken the part of me that was full of motivation. Would this be my pinky toenail? I thought. "There are two parts of you battling for control," said the man. "One is the child who doesn't care how much you weigh, and the other is the adult who is concerned about how you look and has inspired you to purchase this tape. By the time you finish listening to this tape, you will feel compelled to treat your body with more dignity," said the man. "Compelled to make responsible eating decisions."

After a few more minutes of transactional analysis babble, the man told me to get the black polished stone that had come with my package of tapes, lie down in a comfortable position and close my eyes. He told me to prepare to go into a trance-like state.

"Press your stone between your thumb and forefinger," the man instructed.

I found it hard to believe that a black stone that belonged at the bottom of a well-designed koi pond could prevent me from eating sweets, but this man was, after all, a certified emotional support coach with the diet program. I figured he had to know about other things besides garden landscaping.

The man led me in something he called guided imagery. "Pay attention to your breathing," he began. "Now imagine that your body is a balloon full of air. You're feeling more relaxed than you've ever felt before. Feel yourself deflating as you release the air from within and melt into the surface beneath you."

I'm hungry and I want an ice-cream sandwich, I thought. Then I put the thought of an ice-cream sandwich in a bubble and watched it float away.

"You are beginning to lose contact with your physical self," the man said. "Imagine two people standing in front of you. One is the irresponsible child, the other, the responsible adult."

Had I eaten the last ice-cream sandwich in the fridge? I wondered. Then I put a question mark in a bubble and watched it float away.

"Turn to the adult part of you and imagine that it is reaching out to you," said the man. "Imagine that you are holding hands with the responsible adult part of yourself and pull it closer to you."

If the ice-cream sandwiches are all gone, I can always eat one of the Weight Watchers Sundaes I bought. Then I put a Weight Watchers Sundae in a bubble and envisioned it floating away. I thought that Jill from aromatherapy would be proud of me.

"Now press your stone between your thumb and forefinger," said the man. "Pretend you are looking into a mirror and see your reflection. Repeat these statements to yourself in the mirror: I am now the adult in control of my eating. I like myself so much better now. I feel so much smarter now."

The man said he was going to count backwards from five, and by the time I came out of my trance, I would be fully committed to the adult part of me, but that I could always carry my stone with me in times of need.

As soon as the man was done droning on, I got up from the couch, went to the freezer and got my sundae. I didn't think I had really been in a trance, but at least I had been able to picture things in bubbles floating away. As I ate my sundae, I contemplated calling the man and telling him that as a result of his program, my inner child was now in control of my life, but I didn't think he'd appreciate it. Instead, I took my black stone and placed it with the other stones at the foot of a bamboo plant I kept in my kitchen.

The rest of the week on the WW plan was easy because I suffered from a terrible bout of insomnia that effectively curtailed my appetite for three days. If I did not lose weight after something like this, I knew I never would. That Saturday I decided to go to the 11 a.m. meeting instead of the one at 1 p.m. I figured there would be more people at that time, and that if I hadn't lost weight, I could hide amidst the crowd. When I got to the center, it was staffed with a completely different set of workers than the afternoon meeting. "Can I help you?" asked a woman who appeared to be in her late fifties and wore thick black mascara.

"Yes," I whispered, hurriedly taking off my sneakers and standing on the scale. I stood there for several minutes trying not to anticipate the worst while the woman jotted down notes on my progress report. When she appeared to be finished, I stepped off the scale.

"Can you step on the scale?" the woman asked.

"Didn't you just ... ? Oh, never mind," I said, hastily getting back on the scale. I peered over the counter trying to sneak a peak at the results.

"Stand back or it doesn't read right," said the woman.

My face got hot from embarrassment and I withdrew.

"Good," said the woman. "You lost two pounds."

You see, I thought. The worst doesn't always happen.

I walked into the meeting room absolutely elated. I recognized the seminar leader from the year before, a sassy black woman named Evelyn. As casually as if she were telling us where she had eaten lunch, she had mentioned to us that she once attempted suicide. I liked people who were forthcoming about their emotional illnesses. It made me feel less different.

"How are we doing?" she asked a large silver-haired man dressed in white.

"It was a tough week. I gained four pounds," said the man.

"It's all a learning process," said Evelyn.

"You got that right," said the man.

"You just get right back on the plan," said Evelyn.

I started thinking that the weight loss process was very much like my quest for help. I moved ahead. I fell back. But overall I was steadily gaining ground. I felt like telling Miriam from the Center for Personal Transformation about my latest epiphany and see if she felt the same way, but I had a sense that I could find others who would understand what I meant.

I took my seat and watched the room fill up. An Indian man in a green shirt, shorts and sandals gazed at a poster of foods worth four points as though it were a map pointing the way to a hidden treasure. An obese woman in red sweatpants and a red World Wrestling Federation T-shirt sat next to a slightly smaller man. A middle-aged woman with a pixie hairdo came in and sat down to my right. She wore blue cotton shorts and a blue striped short-sleeve shirt. She was the weight I dreamed of being.

"How's everybody?" asked Evelyn, getting the meeting underway.

"Great," everyone yelled in unison.

"Anybody upset?" asked Evelyn.

"No," everyone shouted together. I felt like I was at a Sunday morning Baptist revival. I still felt like an outsider, but I reasoned that this was because it was my first meeting with Evelyn.

"Did everyone work on pages ten through nineteen in the *Getting Started* booklet?" Evelyn asked.

"I only read it yesterday, but I lost three pounds this week," said the red T-shirt. "I watched my portions and just enjoyed life, enjoyed company, enjoyed my food."

"She's happy, happy, happy," said Evelyn. "Let's give her a hand."

Everyone clapped for the woman.

"Is anyone panicking over July fourth?" asked Evelyn.

"I'm going away for three days," volunteered a woman. "And I know that I'm going to dedicate at least one day to eating."

She looked like she did this frequently.

"How many of you just eat because the food is on the plate?" asked Evelyn, walking around the room like a seasoned motivational coach. A bunch of hands popped up.

"I went to a barbecue yesterday, and I shared a hot dog with my friend instead of eating the whole thing," said a woman.

"That's important," said Evelyn. "And you must enjoy the food you do eat." Evelyn turned to a man rolling in fat. "Talk to me," she said. "How was your week?"

"It was just one crisis after another," said the man. "I'm like a yo-yo. I gained three pounds, lost two, then gained four back."

"Now what do you have to do to get back on track?" asked Evelyn.

"I don't know," said the man. "When I have a problem, I eat cake."

"This program is not about food," Evelyn stated emphatically. "It's about why you are eating."

"I'm eating because my daughter is marrying an unemployed ditch digger," said the man.

"Is eating going to solve that problem for you?" Evelyn asked sharply.

"No," whimpered the man.

"We have to face our problems without relying on food as a crutch," said Evelyn. "You can come here for all the support you need."

"A friend told me that I don't look like I'm losing weight," blurted the red T-shirt, "and I had to tell her that I was."

"Why do you feel like you have to defend yourself?" asked Evelyn, putting her psychotherapist's cap on.

"Don't tell anyone you're in WW," chimed in the woman who was already the weight I wanted to be. "I didn't even tell my husband because then he would just say, 'Oh, you can't eat that.'"

"That's a good idea, but my husband's right here," said the red T-shirt, pointing to the man sitting next to her. "He's obsessed with my eating."

"I can be obsessive about eating," confessed the woman who was the weight I wanted to be, in a hushed tone.

"Why do you think you fixate on eating?" asked Evelyn.

"I love carbohydrates," said the woman, with deep conviction.

I looked carefully at the woman who weighed what I wanted to weigh. Was it possible that she, too, felt fat and so she thought she was fat, when this actually wasn't the case? Did she use the same emotional reasoning that Miriam and I had used at the Center for Personal Transformation? Suddenly, I felt like contributing.

"I love carbohydrates, too," I piped up.

"I'm not telling you to give up the food you like," said Evelyn. "There are no forbidden foods in this program. If you love pasta you just have to learn how to eat it."

At this point, the red T-shirt's husband spoke up. "We had a situation this week where we went into the city for dinner," he said. "She couldn't have ice cream because of the medication she's on, so I said, 'If you can't have it, I won't have it either.'"

"And how did that make you feel?" asked Evelyn.

"Good about myself," said the man.

"Medication can be tricky," said Evelyn, "but if you have to be on it, you have to be on it."

All of a sudden and without warning, I said, "My medication makes me hungry."

"What medication are you on?" asked Evelyn.

"I'm on antidepressants," I said, instantly regretting it.

"We can get you off those things," said Evelyn.

I thought I heard the room grow silent and I shrank in my seat. Was everyone staring at me or was it just my imagination? Were they all thinking that I was a total nut job because I was on this medication?

Then I countered with: You don't know what people are thinking unless you ask them, so don't jump to conclusions.

But time, for me, stood still and I was totally unaware that the meeting continued around me. After a few seconds, I furtively glanced around the room to see whether, in fact, anyone was staring at me, but nobody seemed to even notice me.

"I like to look at food when I eat it," a heavy woman in lavender sitting beside me said. "And I like to eat the ingredients while I'm making a sandwich."

"That's a BLT," said Evelyn. "Bites, licks and tastes."

"How can I stop doing that?" asked the woman earnestly.

"I have a friend who wears a surgical mask when she prepares meals," said Evelyn. "And I also know someone who puts Vaseline on her lips when she's making a dish."

There was a smattering of nervous laughter, but Evelyn had fixed her gaze back on me.

"How did you do this week?" she asked.

"Well, it's my first week and I lost two pounds," I said. I expected Evelyn to revisit my mention of antidepressants, but instead she just clapped for me, and the rest of the group followed suit. This gave me a little more courage, so I went on to tell them that I allowed myself one WW ice cream at night, and that apart from that, I reserved the evenings for fruit and vegetables.

"You see," said Evelyn. "She's not depriving herself. She's living the program."

Everyone clapped again, but was it, I thought, out of pity?

I knew that in the weight loss quest, I should stay focused on the process and not be unduly influenced by the readings on the scale, but I felt so elated for losing the two pounds that I went grocery shopping directly after the meeting and uncharacteristically bought bottled water, wheat crackers and carrots for the upcoming workweek. The next morning, as I munched away on my healthful goodies, I thought I heard surrounding co-workers groaning. I went to the newbies board at the Weight Watchers Web site and wrote the following message: "Has anyone noticed that healthy foods like carrots and whole wheat crackers are really noisy? I think my co-workers are going to have me removed from my cubicle if I continue to eat them."

"It seems like the better it is for you, the noisier it is," someone with a screen name of Abyss wrote back. For the remainder of the week I strategically ate my low-points foods when my co-workers got up for meetings and went to the bathroom. At the same time, I tried not to deprive myself of some of the foods I liked to eat. I was doing well until that Wednesday, when my yoga class was cancelled and the friend I took it with suggested that we go out for pizza instead.

"I can't have pizza," I told her.

"Then we won't have pizza," said my friend.

"Wait a minute," I sniped. "Are you telling me that I can't have pizza?"

"You just told *me* that you can't have pizza," she responded.

"Well, I can have anything I want," I retorted. "I'm not on a diet. I'm on a program."

We had pizza.

As I approached the scale the following week, my stomach fluttered the way it did just before I had to give the commencement address at my sixth-grade graduation.

"One," said the scale lady after I had stepped on.

"I gained a pound?" I whimpered.

The scale lady nodded.

Thoroughly dejected, I walked into the meeting room and took my seat in the back row. I should have lost weight, I thought. Then: Why do I think I should have lost weight? A lot of other people hadn't reported weight loss in the last session. I noticed that some of the same people from the last meeting were having a heated discussion about shepherd's pie.

I gained! I wanted to shriek.

The woman who was the weight I wanted to be came in and sat next to me again. She looked over at me and nodded. She had soft brown eyes and a warm smile, so I said, "Hi."

"How did you do?" she asked sympathetically.

"Oh, not too good," I said.

"Me either," said the lady.

Somewhat reassured, I smiled back.

The lady was silent for a moment. Then she said, "What anti-depressant are you on?"

"Elavil," I said, my throat going dry.

"I'm on Prozac," she said.

"Does it make you hungry?" I asked her. Gee, there really are people out there like me, I thought.

"No, it gives me insomnia," said the woman.

"I guess it's always something," I said. I felt like an anvil had been lifted off my shoulders. After my hospitalization I had wanted to take a newspaper ad out to tell the world what had happened to me. Dr. Trieste had gently urged me not to talk about it unless someone else brought it up first. Consequently, only my closest friends knew about my illness. But there had always been something inside me that wanted others to know. Now that I had let a stranger in and she turned out to be on medication too, I realized I wasn't such an oddity after all.

Imagine that.

Chapter 7

Me, Myself and I

The thing about depressives is that no matter how much progress we make in battling our illness, we remain more self-absorbed than the average person.

Example.

The other night my friend Marie called. She was physically and emotionally drained. Before leaving work for a two-week vacation, her boss had said, "Have a good time because you're doing a lot of overtime when you get back." The next day she had adopted two feral cats to join another stray she had previously taken into her one-bedroom apartment. The two new cats had begun howling to be let out in the wee hours. She had gotten maybe three hours of sleep a night. She was afraid her landlord would find out about the cats and evict her. She was quite reasonably scared that she would have nowhere to live with them.

Marie had a divorced friend who was in an even worse space. Marie had to take the woman to apply for welfare because the woman's ex had cut her off completely, and she was too physically and mentally disabled to hold down employment. If she got evicted from her apartment, the woman would have nowhere to live. They sat in the welfare office for seven hours, the woman in tears because she felt that going on welfare was so demeaning. It took Marie all day to get her to fill out the paperwork.

"There but for the grace of God go I," Marie said to me. "I have no one to take care of me either, and no money."

On top of that, Marie's apartment house neighbor, an emotional disaster area, had picked yet another fight and had screamed at Marie, the sweetest and most reasonable human being I knew, on the phone for half an hour.

"She was out of control," Marie said. "And she wouldn't even listen to me."

To anyone with a heart, Marie's problems would have been seen as serious enough to merit a supporting shoulder, but I, being depressive, was totally focused on myself. Because I had never had my emotional needs met as a child, I had never grown out of the infantile state of believing that I was the exact center of the universe and that everything revolved around me. So I quickly said, "That sucks" to Marie's problems and immediately launched into my own.

Problem #1: A bad date. After repeating Denise's "cancel, cancel" over and over again and getting nowhere, I succumbed to online dating where, in spite of predatory sex maniacs and isolated lunatics, I finally started a correspondence with Sam, a fifty-one-year-old divorced man who seemed relatively normal and didn't have kids. This was a big plus for me as, given my past, I did not want to compete with anyone for a man's attention.

"You said you were born overseas," I said during our first phone conversation. "Where was that?"

"I was born in Malta," Sam said with a distinct but unrecognizable accent.

I knew I had heard of Malta, but I wasn't quite sure why. "Where is that?" I asked.

"Malta is a tiny island in the Mediterranean off the coast of Sicily," Sam told me.

"Oh, you're Italian," I said, recalling an Italian sailor I had had oral sex with on a cruise ship many years ago when I was supposed to be playing ping-pong on the Fiesta deck.

"Yes, but I've been here since 1968," Sam said.

Soon the conversation turned serious. Did I have kids? Sam wanted to know.

"No," I said.

"Have you ever been married?" he then asked.

"No," I replied.

Then what have you been doing all these years? Sam wanted to ask me but didn't. Instead he said, "You know I'm Catholic."

"Are you really religious?" I squeaked.

"No, I just celebrate the holidays," Sam replied.

Oh, good, I wanted to say. I didn't want to be held personally responsible for the crucifixion.

"That was funny what you wrote me on your e-mail," Sam said.

"Well, I just wanted you to know that I have Woody Allen's outlook on life because you said you were looking for someone who was positive and upbeat," I responded.

"He's somewhat bleak, wouldn't you say?" Sam said.

"Yes," I said, impressed that a Maltese knew exactly the right word to describe Woody Allen. I found out that Sam owned his own pest control business and I was eager to find out exactly how one got interested in that line of work. We made a plan to meet for coffee at a local diner the following Wednesday.

Enter my Jewish mother. "Are you coming for dinner Wednesday night?"

"No. I'm going on a date with someone from Malta."

"From where?" my mother screeched.

"From MALTA," I stated clearly.

"Wen, can't you find someone from Lynbrook or Valley Stream?" she said, naming towns near where I lived.

"He doesn't live in Malta now," I said, totally exasperated. "He lives in Massapequa."

"Is he *meshugener?*" my mother asked.

"What do you mean *meshugener?*" I inquired sharply.

"You know. *Crazy,*" my mother said.

"Why would he be crazy?" I responded shrilly.

"I don't know," said my mother, backing down. "He's not crazy?"

"I don't know what he is. I haven't met him yet."

"I think there were some sea battles around Malta," my mother said.

There was no question where I got my negativity from. My mother was a world-class depressive. When I was a child, her silent treatments and crying jags had scared me to such an extent that I was unsure if she was capable of taking care of me. As a response, I became even more demanding at a time when I was getting less and less attention due to my older brother's illness. After he became an internist, my brother offered to give my mother a prescription for anti-depressants, but she refused it. Even after all I had been through, she refused to get into therapy and considered psychology "garbage."

A few nights later, I went online and typed in "Malta." A study-abroad program came up. It turned out that Malta had gained its independence from the UK in 1964, that it was a beautiful island whose inhabitants spoke both Maltese and English, though a lot of them also knew Italian. It all sounded so exotic, I started to get very excited about the prospect of my date with Sam.

"I imagined that I was going out with an international spy!" I gleefully told Marie.

"That sounds promising," she said in a measured tone.

Marie knew my history of perpetually getting my hopes up that my very next date would be "the one," only to be disappointed. Isabel had tried to make me understand that such obsessive thoughts were unhealthy and served only to heighten what she called my "anticipatory anxiety" about the future, but I just couldn't stop myself. An hour later, I was relaxing with a mindless reality television show when the phone rang. It was Sam. He wanted to know how my day had been.

"Oh, pretty good," I said, instantly regretting that I had not said something more interesting like: "Great! I discovered a new continent! Couldn't have been better!"

"Did you get outside? It was so nice," Sam said.

"Yes," I said. "I walked at lunch."

"I mowed the lawn this evening," Sam said. This stopped me cold. Jewish people didn't know from mowing lawns—they had Italian gardeners like Sam for that. Couldn't he have hired an inferior ethnic group to do his landscaping? Maybe there were no inferior ethnic groups. Oh, my God, I thought. I'm going out with one of those men who hang out of slow-moving trucks with the cracks in their asses showing.

"Oh, oh," I stammered. Dead silence.

"So, we're still on for coffee Wednesday night?" Sam asked.

"Yes," I said slowly, coming back to my senses. We spoke a little longer. In the back of my mind I remembered that a book I had read on manhunting recommended ending conversations first, so after a few more minutes I made an excuse to hang up.

"Do I need to call you tomorrow to confirm?" Sam asked.

"No, I'll just meet you at the diner at eight p.m. on Wednesday. Looking forward to it. Bye-bye."

I called my mother before I headed over to the diner for my rendezvous with Sam. Mistake. "If he's wearing a cross, you'll know he goes to church," she said in all her wisdom. Now I also knew where I got my hypersensitivity to being Jewish.

The preparation. Following Barbara's dictates, I dressed in a nice black pants suit, put on lipstick and ate until I was full so as not to be hungry at the diner. I knew what to look for; I had seen Sam's picture on the Web site and was relieved to find out that I wasn't fatter than him. He had a medium build and wavy thick brown hair. He didn't look particularly Italian to me. In fact, with my dark complexion I probably appeared more ethnic than he did.

When I got to the Ocean Reef, Sam was waiting outside. He was dressed to go bowling. Not a good sign. He also looked older in person. His face was rugged and his nose came to a sharp point. He awkwardly shook my hand and we went inside. It was my preference to sit in a booth in a corner, but the hostess seated us at a table in the center of the dining area. We would now be out in the open for all to see. The waitress came over and, trained as she was, right away picked up on the fact that this was a first date.

"Did you eat?" Sam asked me.

"Yes, I'm just going to order coffee."

"Do you know what you want?" the waitress asked, barely concealing her glee at how uncomfortable we were together. Sam and I started to order at the same time. The waitress smirked. Sam wanted to order first, so I let him. Bad manners. After the waitress left there was silence.

"So how did you get into pest control?" I finally asked him.

"Oh, I just started the business twelve years ago and it just sort of grew," he said. "I don't even have to advertise now."

"Great," I said, waiting for Sam to ask me about my line of work. He didn't.

Things got even worse when he asked me what my interests were. "I like to see independent films," I said.

"The foreign kind?" Sam asked.

"Yes, those kind," I said, deciding that it was worthless to provide him with an explanation of the difference between foreign and independent films when he really couldn't use the information.

"And I go to the theater," I said.

"I go to the off-Broadway theater," Sam replied.

"Really?" I said, brightening. "What have you seen?"

"Oh, I don't know," said Sam. "There's a theater in Islip I sometimes go to."

"Islip isn't off-Broadway. It's off-Manhattan," I said. "Off-Broadway is like West 72nd Street."

"Well, I don't know about that," said Sam, shifting uncomfortably.

Silence. Then I asked, "So, what are your outside interests?"

"I like to work with my hands," Sam said.

"With the hands?" I replied. "Oh, very interesting."

"I built a playhouse out of wood," said Sam. "It had electricity and running water and a fireplace. It would have cost several thousand dollars to buy."

"Oh? And was that for you?" I stuttered.

"No. For a friend's kids."

More silence. Why couldn't his friends just fucking buy a playhouse?

"And I build computers," Sam said.

"What do you mean?" I asked. "Like a whole computer?"

This date is crashing and burning.

"Yes, I buy the parts on eBay. I can put a whole system together for five hundred dollars."

"That's great," I said. I couldn't think of anything more interesting to say because the concept of building a computer from scratch was alien to me and I had no frame of reference for it.

"Where have you lived besides New York and Los Angeles?" Sam asked.

"Boston," I said. "I've seen most of the United States. I've cruised the Caribbean and been to Nice and Rio de Janeiro."

"What did you think of Rio?" Sam asked, getting somewhat animated.

"I don't really remember it too well. I was young," I said. (The only thing I could remember was my sister-in-law eating a spicy shrimp dish and throwing up in the elevator of the Marriott we were staying at.)

Sam ordered two refills of decaf. I toyed with the yogurt I ordered. He carefully sliced his crumb cake.

"So you were engaged?" he asked me.

"Yes," I said cautiously, "but I wasn't in love with the man, so we broke it off."

"I married someone I wasn't in love with," Sam said.

"Really?" I asked. Welcome to the dysfunctionals club.

"Yes, I felt sorry for her because she had mental problems," Sam continued.

I felt like I had been slapped in the face. I wanted to shout, I have mental problems, too! After all, I could see that Sam lived in a very simple black and white world and was not ready for the complications that a depressed Jewish woman could introduce to it. While I was mulling this over, Sam said, "Her stepfather was Jewish."

Are you a Mussolini sympathizer? I wanted to ask.

More silence. Sam asked for the check. An hour in and it was over. The next day I was horribly down.

"My date was a bomb," I told Marie.

"It didn't sound *so* terrible," she said.

"Oh, no?" I said. I went on to tell her how I had been planning on getting married to Sam in a chic ceremony on Malta, followed by years of living blissfully on Long Island. At some point I would have come up with a pilot for a sitcom based on our years together. We would have moved to Los Angeles and made millions in television. Then we would have retired to Palm Springs and maybe built a huge house in the Hamptons, where we would have invited her over the summer. Now none of that was going to happen.

"My whole life has been taken away," I cried to Marie.

"I wouldn't say that," said my friend.

Afterwards, it occurred to me that this was just another example of my "all or nothing" thinking. Either a date was marvelous or a resounding failure. In this case it was the latter.

Problem #2: I had gotten an e-mail at work from someone in the marketing department. It said, "Please revise your copy to look more like the sample I am enclosing." I had interpreted this to mean, "You worthless, untalented, insignificant hack, change this copy or you will be thrown out on your ass." Let me explain the full history here. The vice president of creative operations had taken pity on me and transferred me to a writing position with the Internet marketing department, which covered all of our book clubs. My new supervisor, Hugh, was a sweet, silver-haired homosexual man who marched through the halls like he was leading a gay pride parade.

"The marketing department really likes it when we're enthusiastic and ask a lot of questions," Hugh had told me when I was transferred to his watch. I immediately thought that my new supervisor had somehow found out about my lackluster interview and subsequent browbeating from the vice president of creative operations. Maybe she told him that I was a nattering nabob of negativism. Maybe she told him that I should be watched carefully. Maybe she planted a recording device in my jacket pocket when I wasn't looking. Maybe … well, you get the picture.

Furthermore, anything that smacked of "new" to me conjured up images of misery. A change can either be good or bad and I naturally assumed that it would be bad. Therefore, I was not big on change and took to it about as well as a golden retriever takes to being ignored. In addition, I was wary of the marketing department, which our department (creative) had to report to. Several MBAs had told me that the dumbest people in business school always went into marketing, and nothing I had seen had convinced me otherwise.

Despite these reservations, things had started out well. I wrote an e-mail to be sent to potential customers and marketing wrote back, "Good stuff." I was asked to do another e-mail along the same lines. I thought they were going to different customers, so I barely changed the first sentence of the e-mail. The next day, I got a snippy e-mail back from my twenty-something contact in marketing. It said, "This is the same exact sentence you had in the other e-mail. We can't use this. We need something fresh." I had been crushed.

"I guess I'm a bad person," I said to my mother later that night.

"You are not a bad person!" she shrieked back. "What makes you think that crap? That is ridiculous!"

Then I started thinking that I was an even worse person because I had thought I was a bad person. I left my mother's on the verge of tears.

The following week at work, I got another assignment. I did it to the best of my ability.

"This is way too long. We need it shortened to half a page," marketing wrote back. I rewrote it and got another e-mail from them. "This is way too short. We need it lengthened to a page." That evening, I went to Isabel in tears. "You're taking this very personally," she said.

"Yes," I replied. "It is personal."

"I'm not saying you shouldn't feel bad about it ..." my therapist said. I waited for her to complete her sentence with "but you're really making an ass of yourself." She didn't. She tried to help me realize that the reason I was taking it so badly was because I had never been able to please my father. (Somehow everything could be traced to that.) "But you're not in a parent-child relationship now," Isabel said. "And this woman who is dissatisfied with what you've written is accountable for telling you specifically what she wants."

I went into my supervisor's office the following day and told him that it would be really nice if we could talk to Ellen, the High Priestess of Marketing, who offered us her commandments through the twenty-somethings.

"Oh, we can't meet with Ellen. She's always in meetings," my boss said. Later that day, one of the twenty-somethings was sent down to our side of the building to appease us.

"What exactly are you looking for in this e-mail?" my boss asked.

"We're looking for more, more ... just more," the twenty-something said as she had before.

About two weeks later, we had started having Friday afternoon meetings in Ellen's large office. This turned out to be a weekly ass-kissing ritual in which Ellen would say something terribly unfunny and everyone in my creative group, *sans* me, would smile and laugh. We would show Ellen our work on the computer and she would say things like, "Nice, nice," and then send us vitriolic e-mails about the work later. Often, in these meetings, Internet marketing terminology would be bandied about by all the twenty-somethings. Not having any idea what they were talking about, I would sit there looking stupefied until someone addressed me with a question, at which point I would sit erect and say, "What?"

About one week after our third or fourth meeting in Ellen's office, I was called in to see my boss's boss, an executive creative director. She was a striking woman who could manage to be both pleasant and aloof at the same time. "This is a part of my job I don't enjoy," she said. "There's been a formal complaint lodged against you."

"For what?" I asked, like a lamb being led to slaughter.

"The marketing people say your writing isn't promotional enough."

Do I get my hands chopped off for that? I wanted to inquire.

"This has nothing to do with your writing ability," my immediate boss piped up. I loved him. As far as I was concerned, he was the one bright spot in this debacle. "You're a very intelligent writer," he told me.

"Then what is it?" I wanted to know.

"You don't contribute much at the Friday afternoon meetings," my boss's boss said.

"I don't contribute because I don't understand what they are talking about," I said matter-of-factly. This is an ambush, I thought.

"We have that problem, too," my boss's boss replied, "but you have to take risks."

"Oh?" I said, for the first time noticing that my heart was pounding as fast as a condemned man's.

"They're giving you a month to turn things around," she told me.

"Okay," I mumbled pitifully.

"Use this month to learn all you can about marketing on the Internet," my boss's boss said. "Ask to see some of Todd's samples, because he's got a handle on this." Then they quickly ushered me out of the office as though they were my parents and I had just confessed to having herpes.

As soon as I got out of the executive creative director's office, I ran back to my desk and phoned my mother. "I'm getting fired!" I yelled.

"What is this shit?" my mother said. As you have probably gathered, my mother was not one for sympathy. I couldn't remember her ever saying anything comforting to me when I was a child, much less an adult. And when I would call her on this, she would immediately cut the conversation short with her patented, "Don't aggravate me!"

I related the story to my mother nevertheless. "Oh, Wen," my mother said, as though I had just told her I had been diagnosed with something fatal. Far be it from her to say something positive in rebuttal.

"I'm quitting," I said. I had a vague memory of reading that depressives give up very easily without searching for different solutions to their problems. I was just following a time-honored tradition.

"You're not quitting!" my mother said, getting agitated.

My last depression had occurred after a lengthy period of unemployment, and all the mental health professionals I had seen since had told me that a depressive needs structure in her life. She needs to get up and go to work every day.

"I'm quitting," I reiterated to my mother.

"You don't quit a job. You make them fire you," my mother yapped, with all the empathy of a woman who had never worked a day in her life.

Over the course of the next few days, my boss did not e-mail any new assignments from marketing. I sat at my desk paralyzed with fear. Should I ask for more work? No. I probably will do a bad job at it. On the other hand, I'm so bored.

"Wouldn't it have been better to show them you were eager for more work?" Marie asked at this point.

Marie, as usual, made perfect sense, but that was not what I had done. I made an emergency appointment with Isabel.

"I need your permission to quit," I told her.

She shook her head. "No. I think this is something you have to work through just like you did on your last job," she said. "If you take the easy way out, you won't grow."

I don't want to grow. I just want to escape this pain.

Back at work. Todd, the other copywriter in my group, was highly uncomfortable with women and spoke to me in grunts rather than words. "Can I see some of your samples?" I asked him.

"Uh," he grunted.

When I got Todd's samples, I realized that the only thing missing from my work was the sentence, "Get 5 books for $1." I, you see, had been thinking of more discreet ways to sell our book clubs, but apparently the marketing whizzes had determined that we had to trick our prospects into becoming members with an enticing offer. I started writing "Get 5 books for $1" whenever and wherever I could, and lo and behold, the marketing people slowly came to the conclusion that they liked my writing.

"You hit a home run," my boss enthused to me one day after marketing accepted two of my e-mails with very little revision required.

"Ah, it was nothing," I said, as nonchalant as I could be. Since that time, I had gotten work back with minor revisions, but I still felt that every e-mail I got from marketing asking for changes actually screamed at me instead of politely requesting. With the latest e-mail asking for revisions, I was again back to being extremely sensitive to rejection.

Problem #3: A British book publisher turned down my book. My agent wrote to me to tell me that the publisher liked my writing and thought I was quirky, but that the book wouldn't work in the English market. I was devastated. I had been with my British agent for six months and our only communication was through e-mail. It was quite possible that he had been writing me on a terminal made available to the patients in the rec room of a British insane asylum.

"Just give him a chance," Marie said.

"I'm giving him six more months!" I insisted.

"You don't have to threaten *me*," Marie said.

Problem #4: My dentist was leaving. The owner of his practice would not make him a partner, so he was starting his own practice at a location that was inconvenient for me to get to. I knew the owner of the practice and liked him, but I was again devastated about the change.

I timed it. I had spent twenty minutes talking to Marie about my problems, while she had spent a mere seven minutes talking to me about hers. I attributed my self-absorption to not having been permitted to tell my parents about my problems as a youngster. My mother had looked at me and seen only herself and her own problems, chief among them that she did not want to be a suburban housewife and had signed on only because it was something women of that generation were supposed to do. (My mother was very bright and was about to enter a Ph.D. fellowship program to study Spanish when she met my father and got married instead.) My mother had no room for my desires and feelings in her life. I had adapted to her wishes by doing away with them, only to find them now bubbling to the surface in all my adult interactions and overwhelming everyone who had anything to do with me.

After I got off the phone with Marie, I made a promise to myself to be less self-absorbed. That lasted about five minutes. I then started obsessing about why my beloved cat no longer slept in bed with me every night. I called Marie back with this complaint.

"It's nothing I would be that worried about," she said.

I had called my friend Joan for support after the date with the man from Malta. Joan was a volatile Italian who liked to try to beat the depression out of me. She lost patience with me and lectured me about how I never gave anyone a chance and was too picky and found inconsequential reasons to reject men.

"Your relationships never last longer than a first date!" she stated. "What is that all about?"

It's about how I want to reject before I am rejected!

I was deeply wounded by her assault and wrote her as much in an e-mail. "Do I attack you on issues you're sensitive about?" I had asked.

Joan wrote me back to say that she was stunned by my e-mail. She had only been trying to help. "It's very difficult for a friend to listen over and over again to the same complaint when she can see the solution to the problem," she wrote. "If you're so sensitive that you don't want me to bring up certain issues, I won't. But that cuts down on the conversation topics, doesn't it?"

"Sometimes when you're really down, it's nice to have a friend who can just listen," I simply wrote back.

"Okay. I'm sorry," Joan wrote me.

"All is forgiven," I wrote back. Then, to break the ice, I asked if she had been in contact with my agent about her brother's book.

"Yes, I have," she wrote back. That was it. Such reticence was highly uncharacteristic of Joan, so I assumed that she had been insulted by my rebuttal and that we were in yet another fight. Joan and I fought often. During my first depression, I had another Italian friend from college who looked alarmingly like Joan. Dr. Trieste had made me realize that having this particular friend was like wearing a hair shirt, a highly uncomfortable garment the monks in the Middle

Ages used to wear to remind themselves of the suffering that Jesus had endured. Why would I do such a thing? he had asked me.

"Because I'm trying to punish myself because I really don't like myself," I had murmured. Was Joan yet another hair shirt?

The next day, I came home to my answering machine with a message from Joan.

"Hi, it's me," the message said. "I started reading your book, and it is very funny."

This, I assumed, was the end of my fight with Joan. Maybe Joan wasn't a hair shirt after all. Maybe this was yet another cognitive distortion, as Isabel liked to call the way my brain had a tendency to misinterpret reality. Nevertheless, I decided to compose a list of things for Joan that she should never say to a depressed person such as me.

They included:

Will you stop that constant whining?
I thought you were stronger than that.
Pull yourself up by your bootstraps.
There are a lot of people worse off than you.

Things Joan could say to me included:

It will pass. We can ride it out together.
Hey, you're not crazy.
I understand your pain and I empathize.
You are important to me.

I put the list aside to present to Joan when she was in a good mood.

That night, my mother and I went to dinner with my eldest

brother and sister-in-law. My brother was good. He called me every few days and nervously asked how I was feeling. I invariably told him that I was feeling fine because if I said I felt like sticking an ice pick through my brain, I was reasonably certain he would have no clue as to how to respond. It was my guess that his greatest fear was that I would have another depression and that he would be in charge of it since my father was no longer around.

My brother and most of his friends belonged to country clubs. From their perfectly coiffed hair to their pedicured toenails, the women who were members of country clubs were so well put together and energetic that just looking at them made me tired. Every time we went to my brother's club for a meal, I had to wear a smile so fake I wasn't sure why my face hadn't cracked.

For the past three years, the "clubbers," as my mother refers to them, had been deliriously happy about their kids getting married. At our dinner, my sister-in-law announced that the Fleckmans' daughter had gotten engaged one day after the Shapiros' son and that the respective weddings would be within one week of each other.

"We've got four weddings in September, three in October and two in November!" enthused my sister-in-law.

"And we've got the Steinmans' son's wedding next Saturday," my brother contributed.

"No," said my sister-in-law. "Next Saturday is the Steins' daughter's wedding. The following Saturday is the Steinmans' son's wedding."

Having to go to all these weddings would have been an unendurable burden to me, but my brother and sister-in-law lived for social things like these.

Now, at the dinner, my sister-in-law, chairman of the golf committee at the country club, told us that she had been yelled at earlier in the day by two eighty-five-year-old women who didn't like their starting times at the club championship.

"One told me she wanted to go off with the A players," my sister-in-law explained, "but she's a C." I wondered how my sister-in-law could remain unfazed by pettiness like this, because it would clearly have been the beginning of an ulcer for me.

I had barely sipped my second cup of coffee when my brother finished paying the bill and announced that it was too noisy and time to go. In addition to the disquieting conversation, I also had not discussed my recent bad date or job troubles with my family; I felt that they were so far removed from these things, they would never be able to relate. This lack of connection was a constant source of pain to me and I often wondered if I had been switched at birth. Were there some depressed bohemians out there mourning my loss? I decided to call Joan despite our spat.

"I just went out with my family," I reported.

"How terrible was it?" she asked.

"I told my sister-in-law that my cat had just turned six and she squinted at me."

"At least she didn't spit at you," Joan said.

"At least," I said.

After I spoke to Joan, I decided that I had to seek out even more people with whom I had things in common and could feel at ease. Perhaps, I thought, I could find others like me back at a Smokers Anonymous meeting, where participants spoke the truth about their nicotine struggles. I hadn't been to a meeting in close to a year but I had recently worked myself down to the lowest-dose nicotine patch—the size of a postage stamp. I hoped to become completely nicotine-free for the first time in two years.

The following Wednesday I drove to the hospital and headed over to the room where the last meeting I had gone to was held. It had been turned into a cardiac rehabilitation center and was full of elderly male heart patients working out. A calendar posted on the wall directed me to a place called the Boardroom. When I found that, I saw that it was filled with people from Alcoholics Anonymous. I was about to give up my search when I noticed a woman walking down the hall who had been present at my last meeting.

"Excuse me," I said. "Are you with Smokers Anonymous?"

The woman, Alice, was startled. She obviously did not remember me.

"Yes," she said. "It's in the basement."

I made my way downstairs and there, seated at a small table, was Hank, the affable man I remembered to be the group's leader.

"Hi, Hank," I said, taking a seat.

"It's good to see you," said Hank, handing me a Xeroxed newspaper article. Seated to my left was an obese old man wearing green shorts and a multi-colored striped shirt. I remembered him from my last meeting, too. Harvey was his name and he used a cane to ambulate. He reeked of body odor. Soon Alice came down with another elderly gentleman named Pete, both carrying coffee cups. Hank gave the articles to the three of them and began our meeting with the Smokers Anonymous pledge, which welcomed everyone regardless of whether they smoked before and/or after a meeting.

"That's us," said Alice.

It was inconceivable to me that Alice, Harvey and Pete had all been religiously going to the SA meetings over the past few years and just as religiously had continued to smoke. Hadn't they gotten the message that the program was simply not working for them? Or possibly they were just lonely and looking for a place to unburden themselves.

We took turns reading the article, which was entitled, "How to Make Yourself Do What Is Good for You." When it was Pete's turn to read, he consistently stumbled over two-syllable words and practically shouted his sentences. I was sure he was deaf. To make matters worse, Alice would correct him, at which point he would yell, "WHAT?"

After we had finished reading the article aloud, Hank said, "Let's talk about fear as a motivator."

"It doesn't motivate me," Alice said.

"Did I ever tell you about my back pain story?" Hank asked me, pressing onward.

"Oh, Jesus," said Alice, and left the room.

"No, I don't think you told me that story," I said to Hank, who proceeded to tell me how one day his secretary told him she was going to the doctor for back pain and a week later she died from lung cancer.

"And my doctor sent me to get x-rays and blood work. And when he called with the results, he said, 'Hank, Hank.' And I said, 'What, what?'" Fortunately, Hank did not have lung cancer. He had also not had a cigarette since.

Alice returned to the meeting room. "I'd like to say something," she said. "I'd like to say that I don't want to live past age eighty-five."

"Oh, don't worry," said Harvey. "You'll be dead way before then, but it won't be from lung cancer. Something else will get you."

Alice somehow did not look comforted.

Suddenly, and without warning, Pete screamed, "YOU DON'T GET CANCER. THE CANCER CELLS ARE ALREADY IN YOUR BODY AND THEY ATTACK THE GOOD MOLECULES."

"Well, I don't know the exact mechanics of it," Hank back-pedaled.

"AND WHAT ABOUT ALTERNATIVE THERAPIES?" Pete screamed. "THERE'S ALL KINDS OF WAYS TO CURE CANCER WITHOUT THEM CUTTING YOU."

"Why are we discussing treating cancer?" said Hank quietly.

"We're here to talk about ways to prevent the need for cancer treatment."

At this point Pete belched.

Hank could see that this was a lost cause, so he turned to me. "How have you been doing, Wendy?" he asked.

I eagerly launched into my whole story about how I was afraid to get off the lowest level of the patch. "But I haven't actually had a cigarette in about two years," I concluded.

Everyone clapped and Hank gave me a high five. "I think the lowest level is only like two cigarettes a day," said Hank. "You can get off it."

Hank went on to give me a few tips on resisting cravings, particularly those I would get in the mornings before heading to what I surmised would be another horrible day at work.

"I want to see you patchless next week," Alice said to me as we concluded the meeting with the "Serenity Prayer."

"I'll try," I said. Pete belched again and it took Harvey ten minutes to get up out of his seat, during which time his body odor was so pungent I actually sneezed twice.

These were my comrades in nicotine. But cigarette smoking was just one of their problems.

I was sad. Most of these people were sadder.

Chapter 8

Bouncing Back

When I was in the hospital, I heard a legend about a kid named Bart. He had dropped out of Yale Law School and landed in the same mental institution several years earlier. Why? He had got a B in his Contracts class.

Resilience, or the ability to deal with adversity without becoming overwhelmed by it, is something that most depressives lack. That's because we are not given the proper materials to build resilience as children. We are not encouraged to develop self-esteem, confidence, responsibility or social skills. Therefore, we feel powerless to change our circumstances and overcome obstacles. The only way to battle lack of resilience as an adult is to realize that it is just your mood slowing you down and that you are more capable than your mood indicates.

My reaction to the events that occurred when I was in college was the ultimate example of my own brittleness. Things not working out as planned in Washington DC would have been a minor setback to most of my fellow students. To me it was a catastrophe from which I could not recover.

When I first arrived in the hospital and told Dr. Trieste about the events in Washington and Boston leading up to my institutionalization, he looked at me in disbelief. Even he couldn't imagine how such a benign series of occurrences could break me, but it had. In the ensuing weeks, we would find out that underneath it all was my emotional constipation.

During my ten years with Isabel I had been able to express my feelings without fear of retribution and had learned that I could weather life's changes. Yes, I was stronger now, but I was always worried that major adversity, like my therapist's leaving, coupled with setbacks like I had experienced at work and in dating, might set me off again. I had read somewhere that seventy percent of people who have experienced two episodes of major depression were likely to succumb to a third. Those weren't very good odds.

But then I forced myself to think of the people I had met over the past several months, like Dr. Gerrie from the self-esteem class, Miriam from the Center for Personal Transformation and the Prozac lady at Weight Watchers. I knew reaching out to them had somehow made me feel more capable because I had realized that there were people out there who, like me, faced emotional problems but were able to carry on. In some cases, like the smokers, they were even worse off than me. I was determined to continue to take more social risks and meet even more strangers to find out if the people I had met were an anomaly.

"Why don't you take a vacation somewhere?" my friend Marie said when I told her about my desires. "Maybe something having to do with your writing."

This sounded like a decent idea, so naturally I pooh-poohed it. The following day I thought about it some more because I realized that I had always been on a quest to find out whether writers become depressed or depressed people become writers.

"I'm thinking of going on a creativity retreat," I told Isabel at our next session. "But I don't really want to go."

"Why don't you want to go?" she asked.

"Because I never want to do anything before I do it," I related. New is bad, I thought.

"Did you go to the Smokers Anonymous meeting?" Isabel

followed up.

"Yes," I told her and launched into a description of the participants and their terrible troubles. When I was finished, my therapist's mouth dropped to the ground. "I think you need to find another group," she said flatly.

"Are you making any suggestions?" I asked.

"You need to find a group of professional individuals that you can relate to," she continued. "At a place where you belong."

"I don't belong anywhere," I muttered.

"Do you want to belong?" she asked.

"Sometimes," I admitted.

"Do you think that feeling of not belonging has anything to do with your family?"

"Of course," I acknowledged. "I didn't belong there, so I don't feel like I belong anywhere. But that's just a feeling. It's not the truth."

Isabel looked triumphant. "That's why this creativity retreat would be good for you," she said. "It's a place you can feel a part of."

Isabel was right as usual, and although a part of me hated her for it, the other part of me e-mailed the organizers of the Creativity seminar. A few days later, one of the seminar leaders called me from Paris to tell me that there were still openings in the retreat weekend in New York at the end of September. Soon after, she sent me an e-mail with a list of things I was to bring. The list included:

1. For show and tell: an object that has great importance to you, preferably from your childhood or representative of it.
2. A large artist's sketchbook or spiral-bound pad, with absolutely no lines on the paper.
3. Some black lead pencils with which to draw.
4. A pair of paper cutting scissors.
5. A ruler.

6. A set of colored pencils.

7. An eraser.

8. A glue stick.

9. A pencil sharpener.

Like an excited fifth-grader the day before school starts, I went shopping for my creativity supplies. When I got home, I eagerly sharpened some pencils. It was the first time I had used a pencil sharpener in twenty years. Suddenly, I decided that I would make this seminar into a vacation weekend that I could tell my nieces from California about whenever they accused me of not having a life. I got on the telephone and called up a swanky hotel that had been recommended by the seminar leaders.

"I'd like to make a reservation for September twentieth and twenty-first," I said when a supercilious reservation clerk answered my call.

"And how many are in your party?" he wanted to know.

"Just me, myself and I," I said.

"Do you know anything about us?" inquired the reservation clerk coolly.

I was a little taken aback because I wasn't aware that I would have to pass a hotel history quiz to gain admittance. "No," I sputtered.

"We're in a converted brownstone located in a quiet residential neighborhood," said the man. "We're a very intimate and romantic place."

And does romance come with the room? I wanted to ask. Instead I forked over my credit card number.

"We have a twenty-four-hour cancellation policy," the clerk said. "If you don't cancel within that time period, we put the charge through." He seemed to be intimating that it was about time I told my parents that I was playing a very unfunny practical joke with their credit card and return it to them, but I ignored him and made the reservation anyway, quickly getting off the phone.

A few minutes later I e-mailed Trudy and Jane, two city dwellers I had met at a writers' conference the previous summer, to see if they would like to meet on the Friday evening before the seminar was to start. They wrote back in the affirmative.

I was excited about my New York City adventure up until the night before I was scheduled to take the train in, when my anti-anxiety medication seemed to stop working and I was seized with an all-consuming dread of socializing. In addition to depression and anxiety, I also suffered from social phobia courtesy of my status as the family outcast, which in turn led to my status as a high school outcast, which in turn left me with an intense, almost disabling self-consciousness and feeling of being judged whenever I was around new people.

"Are you ready?" chirped my mother over the telephone.

"No!" I whimpered. "What if my train doesn't come? What if I get pushed onto the tracks by some deranged sociopath? What if I get trampled trying to bring my suitcase up the stairs at Penn Station? What if the hotel lost my reservation..."

"STOP!" yelled my mother. "JUST COMPOSE YOURSELF."

"Oh," I said.

"You always do this," implored my mother. "You want to try new things and then you get cold feet."

"What if a crazy homeless person hits me in the head with a brick on 82nd Street?" I asked.

"What if the second Ice Age comes?" taunted my mother.

That night I had a nightmare that I had missed my next appointment with my psychiatrist and that he had subsequently turned up at my apartment very angry and prescribed all new medications for me. When I told him that the new pills were too large for me to swallow, he snickered.

When my mother came to pick me up to take me to the train station the following afternoon, I told her about my nightmare.

"This is where you get off," she said, practically shoving me out of the car at the station.

A train and terrifying taxi ride later, I arrived at my Manhattan hotel, a charming converted brownstone with an art deco design. I must have looked totally disheveled because my Indian bellman, Mosheef, immediately went and got me an elegant champagne glass full of peach-flavored sparkling water. "If I want to get breakfast tomorrow morning, I can call down for it, right?" I said, before departing for my room.

"We serve breakfast downstairs between seven o'clock and nine thirty," said Mosheef.

"You mean there's no room service?" I asked.

"No, we don't have room service," said Moosheef.

Well, I thought, there went the fantasy about being waited on hand and foot. Moosheef led me up to my room and left after I gave him a tip, telling me that I could call him anytime I needed something. I almost told him that I needed a man to share my room, but didn't want to come across as pathetic.

Apart from its small size, the first thing I noticed about my room was that it was freezing. I went to the air conditioner wall unit and frantically turned dials. Alas, there was no relief. As a last resort I followed the unit's electrical cord and ripped it out of its socket. Next, I went into the bathroom to check out the size of the tub and saw that it was about the same size as the one in my apartment. So much for taking a luxurious Jacuzzi-style bath. I flopped onto the canopied queen-sized bed's white linen sheets and sipped my sparkling water. For a brief moment I felt like Holly Golightly.

About fifteen minutes later I forced myself out of my room and onto the street to meet with Trudy and Jane. It was an effort for me even to socialize with casual friends because I always suspected that they would find out something new about me that they didn't like. As I walked down the street, my pulse quickened and I felt like I had weights strapped to my ankles. However, as soon as I saw my friends approaching, my reservations subsided.

"Are you ready for a drink?" asked Jane, embracing me warmly.

"Not exactly," I said. My friends looked dumbfounded. "It's just that I get heartburn from alcohol," I hurriedly explained, "and I didn't bring my Prilosec with me."

Why do you have to be instinctively negative?

Then I countered with: The world needs worriers to keep it honest.

"Oh," said Jane, whom I suddenly recalled had a predilection for gin and tonics.

"But I can get a diet Coke while you guys have a drink," I offered. Relieved, Jane steered us to a café that she had wanted to try, and we took a table on the street. We ordered our drinks and a plate of calamari and talked about what we were currently working on. Jane, it turned out, was totally absorbed in a new play about two buildings talking to each other, while Trudy was writing a piece about a participant in her writers' group in Florida, "an eighty-year-old new age freak" who had invited everyone to a nude swimming party.

After Trudy and Jane had finished their first gin and tonics, the conversation turned to the lingering effects of the terrorist attacks on the World Trade Center. Trudy told us of an acquaintance of hers who had seen the plane hit the second building from her subway stop, followed by the people jumping to their deaths.

"She's still in big-time therapy," said Trudy. "She's seeing this Jungian who tells her that she'll feel better if she shifts her eyes from side to side."

Then Trudy segued onto another friend, whom she had met at a writers' conference and whose son had slept with a woman who then turned up pregnant. "Then," said Trudy conspiratorially, "he finds out that she's a dominatrix and the baby probably isn't even his."

When Trudy was done with her friends, Jane decided it was time to discuss some weirdoes that she knew, not the least of whom was her ex-husband, who had married a woman half his age with "blonde hair down to her ankles."

"She convinced him to adopt one-year-old Vietnamese twins, and he's sixty-five!" Jane stressed.

"You know when you see an old man walking with young children in this neighborhood you don't say, 'Nice grandchildren,' because you never know," Trudy observed.

"Fuckers," said Jane.

Three-quarters of the way through our meal, I realized that I was quite enjoying myself. Jane and Trudy seemed to be having a good time, too. We reminisced about the writers' conference where we had met and about the people in the little social circle we had moved in during the weekend. Suddenly I realized that I had been part of a group at the writers' retreat and was about to become a part of another group at the upcoming seminar. Here I thought I would never be accepted into a group, but I already have been. I gave myself the smallest of credit.

That night at the hotel I slept fitfully and awakened several times with more nightmares, including one in which my father came to my bedside to declare his romantic love for me. The next morning, instead of heading for a Freudian analyst's couch, I ate a Continental breakfast at the hotel and took off for the seminar feeling exhausted and uncreative. It was a hot September day, and as I walked through the Manhattan streets, my senses were assaulted. There was the sight of a woman in black hot pants walking a snow-white Maltese and carrying a bag of its poop, the exotic smells from a Bangladeshi restaurant and the loud sound of an electric guitar blaring Hungarian favorites at a street fair

When I arrived at the white brick apartment building where the seminar was to be held, I reached inside my tote for the bottle of water I had placed there and found that it had spilled out. My tote and all my creative supplies were now soaked through and through. Gingerly, I turned the tote sideways and saw the water rush out. There was nothing more I could do, so I entered the building with a trail of fluid behind me.

"Are you here for the Creativity Seminar?" a man at the front desk asked.

"Yes," I said. I looked around the lobby and saw about five other people sitting with large sketchpads. I started to get nervous when I realized that some of them knew each other. (In another one of my nightmares, I am in a college classroom and everyone in the room except me knows everyone else.) After a few minutes, the man at the front desk said we could go up to the fourteenth floor. The elevator ride led us to a narrow hallway and we all fanned out in search of 14J. Soon, someone in our party noticed our instructors' names on a door and rang the bell as we stood outside expectantly.

"Welcome," said a man dressed entirely in white linen as he opened the door. He had silver hair pulled back in a ponytail and wore Mephisto sandals. As I entered his hallway, I was bombarded by the smell of oranges. The man introduced himself as Guillermo and led us into an open space that was undoubtedly his living room. The walls were white and the floor was hardwood. A woman appeared, also dressed in white linen, and introduced herself as Tivka. She had a pallid complexion and wore lavender mascara and peach lipstick.

White rattan mats lay around the perimeter of the living room and each of us claimed one. I looked around at the other participants, primarily incongruous looking women of all ages. The fortyish woman sitting next to me introduced herself as Linda. She had an Ivory girl complexion with clear blue eyes and handsome auburn hair. I thought I detected the trace of an accent in her speech, but couldn't place it. Within the space of five minutes we established that she worked as the executive assistant to the president of the college I had graduated from.

"Didn't you guys just get a new president?" I queried.

"We've had four in the past two years," Linda said.

"I know you got rid of that one who stole millions from the university," I said.

"That was exaggerated," Linda responded somewhat defensively.

Well, off to another great start with a new person, I thought. Then I countered with: Give yourself a chance.

When things had quieted down somewhat, Tivka sat in front of us and told us that the class was going to be about "process" not "product," and that therefore we could not fail. This was a major relief to me.

"You're just going to use each other for inspiration," Tivka said. "We're going to see if your mind can play."

We all glanced around rather uneasily as our leader encouraged us to go around the room and introduce ourselves. Linda went after me and softly told the group that though a university is often thought of as place full of ideas, this was simply not the case, and that she was attending this seminar to reconnect with her creative spirit. Obviously, she is just as unhappy about her job as I am, I thought.

The remaining people in the class included two Indian women who were on vacation in New York, a Jewish male high school English teacher, a Dutch woman who had fled Holland during World War

II, a self-possessed woman who was studying female leadership skills for her non-profit organization, a man who was a financial officer for an Episcopalian church and worked as a masseur at night and a girl with high cheekbones who was into computer graphics and loved to "pa-aint" and draw. I couldn't help but think that we were all round pegs that people had continuously tried to shove into square holes.

After we had introduced ourselves, Tivka embarked on an explanation of how she and Guillermo had gotten into the business of charging people five hundred dollars a weekend to say things to us like, "There are images flying all around and sometimes they hit us and other times we grab them." We didn't have much time to think about this, though, because Tivka immediately started us on a relaxation exercise. "I want you to close your eyes and find a quiet space in your mind," she said extremely softly. "Now I want you to concentrate all your tension in your feet. Tighter. Tighter. Tighter. HOLD ON TO IT." Then, softly again: "Now release the tension across the floor and out of the window."

I was surprised to find that I was able to follow along with Tivka because her voice was absolutely mesmerizing.

We did this exercise with several body parts and then Tivka said, "I want you to keep your eyes closed and envision butterflies in your stomach. These are the butterflies of anxiety, fear and tension." Next, Tivka told us to take out our sketchpads and colored pencils and draw the butterflies in our stomach and name them. I took a turquoise pencil and drew several butterflies. Then I wrote Stan, Jerry and Alice over them. I glanced sideways, trying to steal a look at Linda's butterflies, but she was holding her sketchpad in an inconvenient location.

Next Tivka told us to take another piece of paper and draw flowers with long stems. "These are the stems of possibility that come out of your fears," she said. "These are the stems of hopes and dreams.

Name them, too." I considered naming one of my stems Yvonne, after a friend's sister, but wrote "fantasies" instead.

"Now imagine that your hands are held upward and magical birds land on them," Tivka said. "Up, up, up go your hands into the sky," she continued. Following this, Tivka told us to imagine that we were sitting under a tree on a grassy hill, and that we rolled down the hill until we fell into the sea. "But you find that you can breathe under the sea and you walk on the floor of the ocean until you see a house. It's your grandmother's house. Your grandmother asks, 'Where have you been all these years?' Now I want you to tell your grandmother where you've been all this time."

"Thank God it hasn't been anywhere near you," I wrote down. I had never hit if off with my mother's mother. She was a bossy, outspoken woman who had had no inkling of how to deal with a depressed grandchild.

"Now," said Tivka, your grandmother says, 'Grandchild, I have a magical object that will keep you safe.' Write down what that magical object is."

"A blueberry blintz," I wrote down, because when my grandmother came to our house, this was the type of Jewish soul food she would make for us.

"And then your grandmother says, 'I love you with all my heart and soul, but you can't stay here. Take your magical object and walk away with it.'" Tivka became somewhat animated and said, "Now you hear a loud rumble and in front of you is a monster who says, 'Give me that magical object or I will kill you.' Now on a separate piece of paper, draw the monster and then draw your escape route from him."

I picked up another piece of paper and drew a monster that looked like Casper the Friendly Ghost with a gas attack, and an escape route that consisted of a rickety bridge much like the one over the River

Kwai. I was feeling pretty good about my little creations when Tivka announced that we were going to share them with the people sitting next to us. Not only were we to share, we were to share only in a "whisper," said Tivka, because that creates intimacy, which in turn leads to greater creativity. I realized that under Tivka's nurturing eye, I wasn't half as scared to share my thoughts with Linda as I had been with my partner in the self-esteem workshop.

"These are my butterflies," I whispered to Linda, showing her my drawings.

"Oh, they're so colorful," enthused Linda, as though I were an elementary school student showing her work to the teacher for the first time. "What did you name them?"

"Stan, Jerry and Alice," I said.

"Oh," said Linda, laughing. "I named mine obligation, responsibility and pressure."

"Are you a mom?" I asked her.

"Yes, but it's really my job I'm talking about. I'm like a servant."

"Yeah," I sympathized "that's what administrative work is like."

"I actually resigned my position on Friday," said Linda.

"Do you have another job?" I asked.

Linda shook her head no, and I saw she was eager to get off the subject. At least I have a job, I thought.

"What was your magical object?" she asked me.

"A blintz," I said, quite certain that Linda would not know what that was.

"That's so fascinating," she said. "Mine was a rolling pin!"

"Really?" I said, sensing a connection." Did your grandmother used to bake, too?"

"All the time," said Linda. "And I was really close to her. Were you close to your grandmother?"

"No," I said. "My mom and I are more like my grandfather."

"My mom was my monster," said Linda, showing me a picture she had sketched of something that looked like Jabba the Hut.

"Oh, my," was all I could think to say. And here, I thought, was yet another person who had terrible feelings about her mother. I suddenly realized that this was quite common, and that despite all of the resentment I felt toward my mother, I would never have classified her as a monster. I knew that in her heart she had always wanted to do the right thing by me and had done the best she could given her very limited emotional intelligence. Plus, she had always been there for me when I needed her the most.

After we had a few more minutes to share, Guillermo interrupted to tell us that he wanted to talk about a human quality that was now almost extinct—patience. "You send an e-mail to Uruguay and if you don't hear something back in five seconds you become enraged," he said.

Apparently Guillermo did not have the patience to talk about patience for much longer, because he announced that we were now going to engage in a period of show and tell. Punam, one of the Indian women, went first, thrusting in front of us a cowbell used to herd cattle after grazing.

"Each of these bells is handmade," she said, "and each has a different sound."

Is cow shit really sacred in India? I wanted to ask.

Next to Punam was a rugged looking man with curly, dirty blond hair and a deep resonating voice. He showed us a necklace with a lion's face on it that had been given him by his mother when he was a boy. "I've managed to lose a lot of jewelry," he said, "but somehow, this has always stuck around."

"Can you pass it around?" asked the girl who liked to pa-aint.

"Sure," said the man, who clearly did not want to pass his necklace around. When it got to her, the girl who liked to pa-aint said, "I see the tremendous duality here in the lion's face. On the one hand there's aggression, but on the other hand there's fear."

When the necklace came to me, I looked at it long and carefully. It appeared to be one of the trinkets you'd get for seventy-five cents from a vending machine at an arcade. I couldn't read much more into it. Was it possible that there were people on this planet who were even more sensitive than me, I thought, looking at the girl who liked to pa-aint? It must be tough to be that vulnerable.

In the meantime, the masseur, a large gray-haired man in his fifties from Cleveland, Ohio, withdrew a coin, which he said had belonged to his adoptive mother. "My adoptive mother died when I was seven and I had a very distant relationship with her husband. This coin is like a missing piece of myself."

"That's so special," said Tivka.

"It says, 'Millions for defense. Not 1 cent for tribute.' I don't know exactly what that means."

"But it's a part of your youth," said Tivka.

"I had just been denying my whole childhood," said the masseur. "That's one thing I've learned in forty years of therapy."

So, somebody has actually been in therapy longer than me?

"Does anybody have any questions for Dan about the coin?" asked Tivka.

"You've really been in therapy for forty years?" asked one of the Indian women.

Happily, before my turn at show and tell, Guillermo jumped in and told us that we were going to have a working lunch break during which we would be assigned a partner to interview. Once that was done, we would come back and present ourselves to the others as that person. I was hoping I would be paired up with Linda, but through the luck of the draw, I got Dan, the Midwestern masseur. Since I had spent time as a journalist, it wasn't hard for me to slip into interview mode. For the next hour, over his spinach pie and Greek salad and my melted cheese sandwich and fries, I pried the details of Dan's pathetic life out of him. It turned out he was living with and not married to Catherine, the woman he was at the seminar with. He had taken up with her after his twenty-three-year relationship with his wife had gone south. "She really took me down with her depression," said Dan of his ex-wife. "I wouldn't let her do it anymore."

Immediately, as on my date with Sam, I felt that Dan was rejecting me. I was desperate to find out more details about what exactly Dan's wife did to depress him and if I did similar things, but I didn't want to pry.

When it was time to be interviewed by Dan, I stuck to my general résumé and didn't say anything about my depression. Oddly, however, I sensed that Dan himself appeared somewhat depressed. Had he been projecting his feelings of depression onto his wife? Was he all that happy with Catherine? Was he feeling guilty because he took up with her before he actually got divorced? I realized that I would never know the answers to these questions unless I spent more time alone with Dan, but I knew this wasn't going to happen. I decided instead to just watch him carefully.

When we got back to Tivka's apartment, Guillermo took out a small board and scribbled names on it with a marker. These included Carl Jung, Leonardo da Vinci, Joan Miro and Herman Melville. Then Guillermo proceeded to mention interesting facts about each creative genius, the most eye-opening being that Melville got his idea for *Moby Dick* by staring out of his window and seeing the shape of a whale in the mountains beyond his home.

I wish I could be inspired like that, I thought. Then I countered with: You've been inspired by other things. Like the people you've met.

Subsequently, Guillermo asked us to draw a frame on one of the pages in our sketchbooks. "Now close your eyes and draw geometric shapes in the frame," he said. "After that, draw vertical and horizontal lines." I did as I was instructed, drawing three pentagons and a variety of jagged lines. "Now," said Guillermo, open your eyes and look closely at what you've made. What do you see?"

I looked at my sketch and saw a face. "It's a face," I said to Guillermo, as he came around to see what I had done.

"It's a scary face," Guillermo said.

"Well, yeah. Is it that bad?" I asked.

Guillermo flashed an enigmatic smile and moved on to the next person, at which point I started obsessing about whether Guillermo liked me or not. Then I thought: Why should I care if he likes me? I'll never see him again.

When we had completed the automatic drawing exercise, Tivka said it was time to move on to the "interview performances." She tapped Punam, the Indian woman, and Linda to go first. Punam walked to the center of the room and embarked on a performance as Linda that was worthy of Sarah Bernhardt. She was Linda, the impassioned college instructor; Linda, the parent weighed down by her responsibilities; Linda, the frustrated administrative assistant; Linda, the unappreciated daughter. After Punam was finished, we sat in silence absorbing what she had done.

"Wow," said the girl who loved to pa-aint.

"Don't compare yourself. Don't feel like you have to do better than that," Tivka implored. "Just be inspired by Punam's work and take from it what you can to assist you in your own project."

We must have looked skeptical because Tivka immediately added, "Every great artist has stolen. You have to feel it's all right to steal." I was feeling better and better about Tivka.

Next up was Catherine, Dan's significant other, and the Jewish high school English teacher and former actor. "Can we just get a little closer?" asked the high school teacher.

"Sure," said Tivka, gesturing for us to make a tighter circle. Soon, the English teacher began speaking haltingly and seemed to be turning a dangerous shade of crimson. "My name is, um, Catherine and, um, I had, um, two sisters who both, um, died. One had, um, Lupus and she got a bad kidney transplant and, um, the other sister was, um, on the plane that crashed, um, into, um, the Pentagon, um, during the terrorist attack."

My God, I thought. Listen to this story. It makes your family dramas seem anemic.

We next moved on to the female leadership woman who was playing the girl who loved to pa-aint. "I've got a dream job. I get a great salary. I have a lot of responsibility, but something is just not right, because what I really want to do is to pa-aint and draw. And I like to lie on my bed when I do this, and lately I've been writing comics. I have this character called Depression Girl and she walks around with a black ball following her all over the place. It's me and it's not me. Do you know what I mean?"

Another person that Isabel could sink her teeth into, I thought.

Soon it was Dan's turn to be me. I braced myself for his performance and felt my temperature rise a few degrees when Dan took off with, "If you know me, you know that I wrote a script for the sitcom *Family Ties*, and I was very successful and then I came back to New York and started writing plays ..."

When Dan was done, I thanked him profusely. He could have put undue emphasis on the fact that things ultimately hadn't worked out for me as a screenwriter in Los Angeles, or that I was considered the strange one in my family because I was creative. So when it was my turn to do him, I glossed over the fact that he had probably dumped his wife of twenty-three years for a scheming woman half his age. I played Dan as a completely ethical and sympathetic character, and afterwards, he expressed his gratitude.

As soon as we finished the interview exercise, Tivka pronounced, "Do you see how powerful a simple pronoun can be? Just by using the word 'I' you create empathy and identity."

You can also realize that your life doesn't sound half bad, I thought.

It was Sunday morning and I sat outside Tivka's apartment building eating a coconut juice ice-cream bar and thinking about my latest nightmare, which was that my front teeth had somehow become horribly mangled to the point where even the most experienced orthodontist in New York wouldn't take a stab at them. Were those twisted teeth a metaphor for my twisted soul? I was wondering when Linda approached.

"Great breakfast," she said, pointing to my ice cream bar. Coming from anybody else, I would have taken this as a sarcastic comment, but Linda was so earnest, I knew she meant what she said.

"Thanks," I responded. As we took the elevator up to Tivka's apartment, Linda told me about her excursion to the New York Public Library the previous evening to see a structure that had just been erected in the courtyard.

"The juxtaposition of the glass and metal with the classical foundation was just amazing," she said.

At this point I tuned her out because that's what I do to people who drop snobbish words like "juxtaposition" in casual conversation. We took our places on our mats and pretty soon everyone from the day before had congregated once again.

"Society gives us the impression that it's not okay to be creative if we're not making money at it," Tivka said, starting off the second session, "but that's not true. It is all right. You just have to find like-minded people to be creative with."

Well, this bunch of boobs found each other, I wanted to say.

Soon Tivka launched into her relaxation exercises. "Now," she said afterward, "I want you to close your eyes and pretend you can see all the way around your heart. Then draw a topographical map of your heart, labeling all the mountains, streams and towns."

I took out my colored pencils and started scribbling mountains that looked like meringue cookies. Next to one of the mountains I wrote Heartbreak Hill. Then I drew a river and named it, the River of Regrets and a lake I called Pity Pond.

"Now I want you to see 360 degrees around your brain," Tivka said. "Then I want you to draw your brain and name all the areas of it."

I took a pencil and drew what looked like a large lima bean. In one section I created a space called Inspiration Inlet, which was surrounded by Creativity Corner. I colored the rest of my brain black and wrote Brain Dead.

"Now I want you to put the drawing of your brain next to the drawing of your heart and show me the path you take to get from your heart to your brain and vice versa."

I drew a path from Heartbreak Hill up to Creativity Corner for my heart to my brain and Inspiration Inlet down to Sorrow Sand Trap for my brain to my heart.

At this juncture, Guillermo took over and had us close our eyes again and imagine that we were walking a few inches above the floor of the Atlantic Ocean heading east. "Now imagine that you have hundreds of eyes all over your body. Eyes everywhere. You can see 360 degrees with all your eyes." Somehow, a few seconds later we arrived in Florence and saw a man in a blue suit approaching us. "Soon you see that this man is actually your father, and he gives you a letter addressed to you from him on your sixteenth birthday. Now I want you to write this letter."

I took my pen and started writing. My letter said:

> Dear Wendy,
>
> Happy Birthday to my beautiful daughter. I'm so proud of you and all you have accomplished, particularly at school where you are almost a straight-A student. I don't really understand how you got that B in algebra. Won't you work a little harder for Daddy, please? I'm an old man and I don't have that much longer.
>
> Love, Daddy

Presently Tivka came back to the front of the class and paired us up for the day's "whispering" exercise, which would be to share our heart and brain sketches and letters from our dads if we wanted to. I was paired up with Catherine, Dan's live-in. As I walked over to her, I surmised that she must have liked my performance as Dan because she greeted me warmly enough. I noticed that she was wearing a frumpy blue checked outfit that looked like it had been purchased at a state fair, and ceramic earrings with beads and little polar bears on them. I thought she looked remarkably carefree for someone who had lost two sisters, but then again, I realized that she was a Midwestern gentile and came from strong stock.

"I think this map exercise was a defining moment for me," Catherine said as I sat down next to her. "I had always thought about the connection between my heart and my brain in the abstract, but this is so concrete."

"Yes, it most certainly is," was the only thing I could think of to say. Catherine went on to tell me that the path from her heart was actually an underground river that turned into a powerful fountain that spurted upward when it reached her brain. Meanwhile, the path from her brain to her heart was a stairway. "That's critical," she said to me, tracing the stairs with her finger. When I showed Catherine my pathways, she laughed heartily.

You see, a Midwesterner can appreciate your sense of humor, too, I thought.

Now it was Guillermo's turn to take over again. "I want you to close your eyes and write down the first word that comes to your mind," he said.

I closed my eyes and wrote down "vegetable."

"Next, I want you to close your eyes again and write that word or sentence over and over again as fast as you can for ten minutes."

We all did as we were told, but about halfway through I opened my eyes to see what my scribbles looked like. Much to my alarm, "vegetable" was going sharply downhill in every new line. I was sure this meant that a handwriting analyst would tell me I had a major character flaw.

"Now," Guillermo was saying, "I want you to open your eyes and circle with a colored pencil your favorite sentence."

I circled one line that had vegetable written across it.

"Next, take that sentence and write about it for five minutes," said Guillermo. I dutifully wrote down, "I hate vegetables even though Weight Watchers says I should eat more of them. The only vegetables I like are carrots and they are too noisy to eat at work. I also like cucumbers, but you have to be careful with them because if you leave them in the refrigerator too long they can grow a disgusting mold that can overrun your whole apartment." (This had actually happened to me.)

When we finished, Tivka came back and told us that this exercise teaches how to edit what you write. "You need to create a jungle of words to save that one, beautiful sentence," she said. Most of the class murmured appreciatively. I looked at my watch because my stomach was starting to grumble. Sure enough, Tivka announced that we would be taking another working lunch break. She paired us up again—this time my partner was Catherine—and passed around a jewelry bag filled with rolled up pieces of yellow paper that had sentences on them.

"You're to take these sentences and draw and write a story around them," said Tivka. I looked down at my paper and read, "She was halfway up the mountain when the rain started."

Catherine and I decided that we would go to a bagel store up the block to grab lunch and brainstorm. Heading up 82nd Street, however, I could barely keep pace with her. She walked with such purpose and confidence, it felt as though she was proclaiming herself to New York.

"I'm into movement," she told me as I huffed and puffed behind her. "Not dance. Movement. I study with Continuum. They teach movement from the inside out."

"Oh, really?" I said. And what planet would that be on?

"You start with your pinky finger and work your way out," said Catherine as we arrived at the bagel store.

Catherine was definitely weird and I didn't want to encourage her further. Therefore, when we walked into the shop, I cut her off by asking what she was going to eat.

"Oh, nothing. I don't eat before four p.m.," she said.

I proceeded to self-consciously order a bagel and sat with Catherine at one of the establishment's small tables. Whenever I did something that the person I was with didn't do, or vice versa, I felt at fault.

"So," said Catherine, brimming with enthusiasm, "She was halfway up the mountain when the rain started."

"And suddenly the mountain gave way," I said.

"And there's a whole city of people, underground people," Catherine continued.

"Little people. And they are working."

"No," said Catherine, as though she had suddenly seen a vision. "They're sewing."

"And they are happy, whistling like Santa's elves?" I volunteered.

"No," said Catherine emphatically. "They are oppressed."

"They're oppressed by Isaac Mizrahi," I jumped in. "And they want to form a union—the International Lilliputian Garment Workers Union."

"No," said Catherine, going full throttle now. "They want to have a support group. Designers Anonymous. DA." Then Catherine laughed at discovering how brilliant she was. After Catherine had shot down all my ideas, we walked back to Tivka's apartment and sat down with a sketchpad. I remembered Isabel talking to me about how when a person feels out of control within, she often needs to control her environment on the outside. Was Catherine's need to control our writing exercise somehow related to the inner turmoil she felt from having two deceased sisters?

"You write and I'll draw," Catherine suggested to me.

"Okay," I said, writing down the sentence we had been given.

"Oh ... oh!" said Catherine, "We have to name our main character."

"How about Guenivere?"

Catherine grimaced. "How about Lizzie? Lizzie Liberator. And she brings the Little People a magic cloak that makes this man you're talking about disappear. Yes, that's it. No. Wait. The cloak gives this person you're talking about a conscience."

"Okay," I said. "So when the Lilliputians see Lizzie they say, 'You're the person we've been praying for all these years.'"

"Can't we be more creative than that?" asked Catherine.

I tried not to take it personally.

Because time was running short, we ultimately became one of only three pairs that got to share their stories with the class. When it was over, I was in a sour mood; Catherine had totally co-opted the telling of our story, embellishing it with details she apparently felt it was beneath her to share with me. Also, one of the other stories was set in a psychiatric hospital, but the partners kept referring to it as "an insane asylum."

It doesn't look like that, I wanted to say.

After the stories, Tivka told us that it was time to take out our homework assignment from the previous day. We had been told to come to class with ten objects that could fit in the palms of our hands. I had taken some things out of my pocketbook and hotel room like coins, pens, medication bottles and Post-it notes. Now Tivka told us that everyone would get twenty minutes to come up with a "play story" about our objects. The stage for the story would be a chair.

I looked at my objects, clueless. Do you have no imagination? I derided myself. But then a story came to mind, revolving around my morning trips to Dunkin' Donuts to get iced coffee.

When the twenty minutes were up, Tivka asked for a volunteer to go first. The Lion's Head man raised his hand and proceeded to enact a play about finding the keys to the imagination with characters that included a paper clip, a match and a poker chip. Along the way, the Lion's Head man quite admirably performed French, British and Bronx accents.

"You should go to Los Angeles and do voiceovers," I told him afterward.

"Already been," he said. "I went back to Chicago."

"Who wants to go next?" asked Guillermo after the Lion's Head man. I tentatively raised my hand.

"Okay, Wendy," said Guillermo.

I brought my objects to the chair. I took my empty bottle of pills and began: "Hi, Dunkin' Donuts. Can I help you?"

Coin: "I want a medium iced coffee with three Equals, very light."

Pen: "I want a large coffee, dark, with one Splenda."

Baggie: "I want a small coffee, half skim milk, half regular milk, extra sweet."

Bottle of Pills to Coin: "Okay, you want one small, dark iced coffee with two equals."

Coin: "No, I want a medium iced coffee with three Equals, light."

Pen: "And I want a large coffee, dark, with one Splenda."

Bottle of Pills to Pen and Coin: "So you want a small coffee with three Splendas. And you want a small iced coffee with no sugar at all."

Pen and Coin: "No!"

Baggie: "I'm changing my order. I want a large coffee, very light with skim milk and one sugar."

As I continued with further miscommunications and entanglements, I heard the sound of my fellow participants laughing.

"This is hysterical," said the girl who loved to pa-aint.

They think I'm funny!

I felt so emboldened by their laughter that I concluded the skit with the Pill Bottle saying: "I can't take this. I'm on medication!"

That got the biggest laugh of all.

"That was great," said Tivka. "Very humorous."

I was elated. I remained that way throughout "Play Time," as no one's story elicited the degree of mirth that mine had.

"Let's take a break and go back to show and tell," said Guillermo after everyone was done.

I was still high when Linda extracted a tiny wooden figurine from a plastic bag. It looked like a Pinocchio on cross-country skis. "When I was a child," Linda began, "we moved quite a lot, so I didn't get to hold on to many things. This is one of the things that moved with me."

"Where did it move to?" asked Tivka softly.

"It was born in Sweden and moved to England and then Canada and then Massachusetts and then New York and then Iran and then New Hampshire and then back to New York."

"Wow," murmured Tivka.

There's a lot of pain in that, I thought.

"Anyone else want to go?" asked Tivka.

Catherine raised her hand and pushed a glass of water forward. "This looks like tap water, but it's actually Lake Erie," she said. "I spent many summers there as a child, and water is a motif in my life."

"I like how you put that," said Tivka.

"When my sister died on flight 77, they found her remains, and we had her ashes scattered over the lake," Catherine continued.

"Do you swim?" the girl who liked to pa-aint asked gently.

"Yes," said Catherine. "It's one of the things I love."

More pain, I thought.

After we all observed a moment of silence, I raised my hand to go. I was now totally feeling part of the group. I reached into my bag and pulled out a photo of myself when I was twelve, holding my golden retriever puppy. I told the group that the photo evoked mixed feelings. On one hand, he was the first dog my family owned that was my dog. On the other hand, my parents had given him away when I went to college and I deeply resented them for it.

"How old was he when you gave him up?" the English teacher asked.

"Three," I said.

"Do you have a pet now?" Guillermo asked.

"A cat," I said.

"If you could personify your pet, who would she be?" asked Tivka.

"She'd be Mrs. Hercule Poirot because she's always investigating," I said.

"That's fabulous," bubbled Tivka.

After I went, the girl who loved to pa-aint passed around a seashell that looked like a skull. "I found it when my mother was dying of cancer," she said. "Everywhere I went I saw skulls. Is that morbid?"

I'd say.

"I think that it's ultimately life affirming," said Tivka.

At the end of the session, Tivka handed out beautiful Italian note cards and told us to write notes to ourselves on them about what we needed to do to stay creative. I took my postcard and wrote, "I need to keep meeting hard luck cases like I've met at this seminar and find out that their lives are worse than mine." I placed my card in an envelope and gave it to Tivka.

"Thank you," she said.

"No, thank you," I said.

Chapter 9

The Glass Half Full

To say that I was a pessimist would be like calling the Mongols unkind. I was a mega-ultra-super-sized pessimist. I was the kind of person who walked out of her apartment expecting airplane parts to fall from the sky onto her head. I was the kind of person who was convinced she was going to come home one day to find that her cat had been murdered and dismembered by an escapee from a local prison. (Never mind that there was no local prison.)

Of course, I had struggled mightily to keep positive about the Creativity Seminar and found it to be quite pleasant and enlightening. I felt I had made great strides, but wanted to continue in this upbeat vein. That's why when I saw a course called "Humor and Learned Optimism," I thought of taking it. This somewhat perplexed my British agent, who was still feeding into my fantasies about my book.

"Humor and learned optimism," he e-mailed. "Hmm, a combination that leads inevitably to wild hysteria. Humor and optimism are not necessarily compatible, not without a brittle edge there somewhere."

Despite my agent's misgivings, I decided to sign up anyway, and on the appointed day arrived at the classroom to find another collection of women arranged in a semi-circle, with our facilitator, Edward, at the front of the room next to a projection screen and his PowerPoint presentation. He looked to be in his late thirties and had thick, wavy brown hair that seemed to be begging for some sort of anti-oil treatment.

"Is this the optimism class?" I asked one of the women.

"Yes," she said.

"You passed the first test," I responded, taking a seat next to her. She laughed at the joke. Presently, two men drifted into the room, no doubt lost, and took their seats in the semi-circle. Edward introduced himself as a psychotherapist and former stand-up comedian who also led a stress-reduction drumming circle. He told us that he had several corporate clients and ticked them off. I made a mental note not to buy stock in these companies.

"The challenge with optimism is that it's okay to have a negative emotion, but that we have to let it go and move on to something positive," Edward began. Then he went into a story about how he had come to the classroom about forty minutes before anyone had arrived and saw that the setup of the chairs and electrical outlets was all wrong for his presentation. "I could have stayed upset about it, but instead I saw the humor in the situation and learned to work around the problem."

I couldn't actually see any humor in the situation, but Edward was already on to his next point, which was that we were going to spend the next two Saturdays "playing with and looking at ourselves and taking responsibility for our thoughts and fears." He prompted us to go around the room and introduce ourselves and tell why we had decided to take the class.

"I take things too seriously," said one woman.

Another said, "I just moved here from Texas and I can't cope."

I also heard, "I have fibromyalgia and I need a little levity in my life" and, from a man sitting next to me who had a thick foreign accent, "I turned to a page in the catalog and this course looked good."

I simply told everyone that I was a pessimist by nature and wanted to change that.

After we had introduced ourselves, Edward put a slide up on the screen that said "What Blocks Humor?"

"Does anyone know the answer to this?"

"Anxiety and tension," said the Texas woman.

"I think it's a learned behavior that we picked up from our parents," the woman sitting next to me said in a tremulous voice.

"Good," said Edward.

"And the media doesn't help," someone else piped up. "Everything on the news is so negative."

"Here's an experiment I want you to try before our next session," said Edward. "I want you to spend one day not reading a newspaper or watching the news on television. How do you think you'll feel then?"

"Uninformed?" I volunteered. A few members of the class chuckled.

"I think fear is another big factor," said the fibromyalgia lady.

"Very good," said Edward. "How many of us can laugh when we're afraid?"

The Joker from Batman can, I wanted to say, but this time held my tongue. I wanted to contribute, but I didn't want to become obnoxious.

"It all has to do with patterns of behavior," Edward continued. "If you think of yourself as a happy, joyous person, that's how you'll act."

I told my agent that I was a pill, I wanted to offer, but didn't.

"And let's also look at the need to be in control," said Edward, quickly clicking through his presentation. "We think that as adults we have to be in control, but laughter comes from being free."

Edward followed this up by reciting a poem called "Through the Eyes of a Child."

"How can we recapture the freedom and joy we experienced as

children?" Edward asked. "How can we skip or go on a swing like children do?"

I thought about my childhood. I couldn't remember any freedom or joy associated with swings. I was always afraid my father would push me too hard and the swing would go over the top bar and I would fall off, land on my head and sustain brain damage

"You have to find support for these feelings of joy," Edward said. "How many of you have friends who lift your spirits?"

A few people raised their hands.

"Now, how many of you have friends who bring you down?"

Many more people raised their hands now.

"I had a friend who was so funny," said the Texas woman. "Then she had a lot of stress, and now she's not funny anymore."

"I know people like that," said the fibromyalgia lady.

I thought of my close friends. They almost always were in the position of lifting my spirits. Maybe that can change, I thought. I can listen more to Marie, fight less with Joan and do more fun things with my friend Elaine.

Edward clicked and another slide came up: "What do we Need to Have Humor?"

"First and foremost we have to have *no blocks*," said Edward. "We have to have a mental frame of mind that values humor as good and important, and we also have to be relaxed."

"Yes, that's very important," said the fibromyalgia lady, giving an unnecessary second opinion.

Edward clicked the lights in the room off and told us he was going to take us through a relaxation exercise called body scanning. I couldn't help but feel that I was back in Tivka's apartment.

"I want you to shut your eyes, sit back in your seats and pay attention to your breathing. Is it thoracic breathing—shallow and quick—or is it deep, long breathing coming from your diaphragm? I want you to breathe deeply and feel your cholesterol going down."

I started to watch my breaths the way Isabel had recommended several months previously.

"Now I want you to feel your shoulders," continued Edward. Are they up or down? Up. Pull them down and relax them. Feel your mouth. Is it clenched? Yes. I want you to part your lips and drop your jaw to relax it." Edward went on like this for several minutes naming, and telling us to relax, each body part. Amazingly, I was able to follow along.

"Now I want you to imagine that you are in a movie theater," he continued. "You are sitting on a cushioned seat, taking in all the sounds, sights and smells of the theater. Suddenly, on the screen you see images that make you very relaxed. What are these images?"

I tried to think of images that made me relaxed and came up with visions of lying on a chaise lounge on a Caribbean beach, sipping a piña colada and of lying on my couch with my cat sleeping on my legs. I tried to replay these images over and over again in my head.

"Now I want you to imagine that on the movie screen there are scenes of joy and laughter. I want you to get up and walk through the screen and into these scenes."

I came up with an image of the time I was at a sixth-grade Halloween party at one of my friend's, and a girl whom I did not like lost a tooth during the apple bobbing contest. I smiled to myself.

"Now I want you to see up on the screen a vision of your ideal self as you would like it to be in the future," Edward said.

I pictured myself leading a class in self-esteem building.

A few minutes later, Edward counted from one to ten, at which point we were supposed to snap out of our trances. This was fairly easy for me as I had not been in a trance. I didn't want to disappoint Edward, however, so I faked a yawn and opened my eyes to see my classmates looking dazed. At least, I reasoned, I had been able to follow along with most of the exercise. "Did anyone feel like they were about to fall asleep?" Edward wanted to know.

"Yes," said the fibromyalgia lady. "It was like I was dreaming."

Maybe in the next relaxation exercise I'll feel that way, I thought.

"Many people have the same reactions to stress," Edward said. "It's either fight or flight because when we were cavemen and the lions chased us, we had to run back to our caves to be safe. The lions aren't chasing us now, but we still get the same physiological reactions."

At the place where I work, I'm sure there are animals chasing me, I wanted to contribute, but realized that there would be time for this later. Besides, Edward was already on to listing sources of stress in conjunction with nifty cartoons and photos. I got the impression that he was way too attached to his presentation materials. Drawing to the close of this section of his seminar, Edward asked us what was the number one factor that caused stress. We were stymied so he placed a pithy quote up on the screen and announced, "The number one factor that causes stress is our perception of events. That means you have the power to determine whether you will be stressed or relaxed."

Suddenly I remembered reading somewhere about a man who had cancer and a friend of his who was perfectly healthy. The man with cancer, however, was more optimistic than the healthy man simply because he perceived himself as lucky that there were treatments available for his type of the disease. At the same time, the perfectly healthy man perceived himself as unlucky just because he had lost some money on a stock he had recently purchased. The article concluded that everyone had an emotional baseline—a level of happiness that you almost inevitably return to after being happy or unhappy. And it was all a matter of perception.

At this point, Edward probably felt that we were ready for some bad news because he launched into a section of his presentation about "stress-hardy" individuals who don't get stressed because they view challenging events as opportunities to grow.

I'm becoming more stress hardy, I thought. Just look at all these daunting classes I'm taking. Even my agent is impressed.

"Say you have an appointment to get to and you're in your car in a traffic jam with no cell phone. How would a stress-hardy individual handle that?" Edward asked.

"He would say 'There's nothing I can do about it, so I'm just going to go with it,'" said the tremulous lady sitting next to me.

"He would listen to a book on tape or music in his car," said one of the guys in the class.

"He would say, 'What is the worst thing that could happen?'" said the Texas lady.

"Exactly," said Edward. "It's the eighty-year-old rule. Does everyone know what the eighty-year-old rule is?"

We shook our heads.

"That means you have to ask yourself, 'Will I remember this when I'm eighty years old?' If not, you let it go."

I can do that, I thought, envisioning myself remaining calm the next time I was on the bowl and realized I had no toilet paper. It might not have been fantastic, but it was a start.

Just as I was tucking the eighty-year-old rule away, Edward started to address "learned optimism" and how we could discover the most helpful aspects of a terrible situation using a process that we were to practice over and over again called "reframing."

"You ask yourself what you can learn from the situation and how you can take something positive out of it," Edward said. He told us each to take a piece of paper and write down a situation or event in our life that we perceived as negative. Then underneath we were to reframe this event/situation in terms of learned optimism and see if we could find something positive in it. Finally, we were to pick a partner and share the negative event and the positive reframing with her and ask for further suggestions about how the event could be construed as positive.

I took a piece of paper and wrote down that the businesspeople I worked with were again unhappy with something I had written. For the reframing I wrote "It's great because it gives me an excuse to shoot myself." I crossed that out and wrote, "It gives me the opportunity to build a thick skin, which will help me in other aspects of my creative writing."

I looked over at the tremulous lady, who was also done writing.

"Do you want to be my partner?" she asked tentatively.

"Sure," I said. I saw that the foreign man did not have a partner, so I invited him to join us too. I went first and spit out my story. Immediately my two partners searched for a solution to my work problems.

"Why don't you ask them what they want beforehand?" the foreign man asked.

"They don't know what they want," I told him. "They only know what they don't want, which is nearly everything I give them."

"Hmph," said the tremulous lady.

"But enough of my problem," I said. "What about yours?"

"Well, I took this sculpture class," said the tremulous lady. "I wanted to make my mother's hands for her for her eighty-fifth birthday, but the problem was that I had never sculpted before and I have no artistic ability whatsoever."

"That could be problematic," I interjected.

"I made the left hand and the teacher said the right hand should be exactly like the left hand, but I just couldn't … I couldn't (at this point the tremulous lady broke down). I couldn't make the right hand," she sobbed. The foreign man patted her on the shoulder.

"At least you tried something new and that should give you confidence to try other new things," I volunteered. I was very proud of myself for what I thought was a positive approach to the situation.

"Yes, that's exactly what I wrote down for reframing," said the tremulous lady, slowly pulling herself together.

"And what you made was your own," said the foreign man.

"Yes, it was your own vision," I said, on a roll.

"Yes," said the tremulous woman softly.

Another hard luck case, I thought.

After we had succeeded in calming the tremulous lady down, it was the foreign man's turn to go. "I work in a place where there are a lot of layoffs," he said. "And they tell me things are changing and I have to do new things or my job will be gone."

"Where do you work?" I asked him.

"In a machine shop," he said.

"Isn't there a union?" I asked, recalling *Norma Rae.*

"Yes, but it's not that strong," said the foreign man.

"Are you Italian?" I asked.

"Croatian," he said.

I didn't know Croatians had problems, I wanted to say. Instead, I said, "It's an opportunity for you to learn some things that you can take to another job if you want to leave there."

"Yes," said the foreign man hesitantly, as though he had just realized that he did not belong in the continuing ed environment. Meanwhile, I was patting myself on the back for yet another appropriate response.

About ten minutes later, Edward told us to wrap up. He then explained that we were going to go around the room and each of us would divulge our negative event and the positive reframing that had taken place. Everyone groaned. A blonde lady on my side of the room went first.

"I do too much at one time," she said. "I'm always saying 'yes' to everybody."

"I've learned that anyone can say 'no,'" the fibromyalgia lady piped up.

"But they give me guilt trips," noted the blonde woman.

"You have to get over guilt," the fibromyalgia lady pressed. "I have Italian guilt. My mother calls me at nine a.m. and asks why I didn't call her today. You just have to ignore it."

"You need to put an affirmation on your mirror that says, 'My needs are important,'" Edward jumped in.

Once we had thoroughly investigated the blonde woman's options, we moved onto the Texas lady, who told us that she was just going to whine.

"You're allowed to whine for a minute," said Edward.

"I hate New York," the woman wailed. "I can't believe I moved here. The apartments are so expensive and they're not even nice and it's so dirty and noisy all the time and the people are really rude."

A chill filled the air. To salvage matters, Edward noted, "But you have to think of the positives, like the great theater and restaurants."

The Texas lady just slumped in her chair.

Next up was the fibromyalgia lady, who told us how traumatized she had been by the diagnosis of her medical condition and how on some days she could barely get out of bed. She told us that the positive side of it was that she had founded a non-profit organization to try to find a cure for the intractable disease, and that she had learned to set limits for demands made on her.

"You see, even in the face of a terrible disease, some positive things can be found," said Edward.

A few more people went with serious problems like near-fatal car accidents and the end of twenty-year romantic relationships, so that by the time it was my turn to go, I felt like terribly small potatoes.

"So you're learning positive ways to cope with difficult people at work," Edward said when I had finished blathering.

"Yes," I lied. I simply wasn't a believer in my ability to reframe the events that happened in my own life.

After the last person had gone, Edward asked us how if felt to share. Everyone, including me, agreed that it felt good. "Just by talking you boost your immune system," said Edward. "Give yourselves a round of applause." Everyone, including me, applauded. And I meant it this time.

Edward then launched into a story about how he had gotten laid off as a legal document processor and that this had somehow led to his nephew's getting a job writing for Fox television. "There's a big picture that sometimes we don't see at the time," he said. "Everything is actually unfolding perfectly."

I racked my brains to try to figure out what the big picture in my life was and how what I was experiencing on my present job was related to it, but Edward was already on to his next topic, which was gratitude. He told us that each of us should write down twenty things for which we were grateful.

"As you write, breathe in the gratitude," he told us. "And think about how you feel. Are you really grateful or do you resent gratitude."

Yes, I thought, writing down a few things. I resent anyone telling me to be grateful.

When our time was up, I realized that I had written down only six things. "Now," said Edward. "We're going to go around the room and each of you is going to stand up and list seven things that you are grateful for. And you're going to say, 'I am grateful for such and such.' There's just an energy, a vibration, when it's shared like that."

As each person stood up, I ransacked my brain for a seventh thing to be grateful for. What could it be? That I didn't step on any cracks in the sidewalk today? That a Bangladeshi man at Dunkin' Donuts gave me a free Munchkin? By the time they got to me, I had come up with "I am grateful for a neighbor who takes my mail in when I am away on vacation." This seemed to suit everyone just fine as, like the others, I got a hearty round of applause when I was done.

There were only fifteen minutes left to the session and I thought I would use the rest of the time to decompress, but this was not to be the case. We had to do one final exercise, which was to write down ten things about ourselves that we appreciated. I came up with nine, and for the last one I wanted to write, "I'm open-minded enough to take ridiculous classes like this," but decided against it in favor of, "I buy great gifts."

"I want you to partner again and give your list to your partner, then close your eyes and listen to her say all the things that are good about you. This time I wound up partnering with the foreign man. I closed my eyes and listened to him say, "Wendy, you are intelligent. Wendy, you have a great sense of humor …" and so on. Then I took the foreign man's sheet and told him, "Roman, you are a good provider. Roman, you are a great father …" and so on.

"How did that feel?" asked Edward. "Did you feel fidgety, like you wanted it to be over?"

No, I thought. Although praising myself was still difficult, it wasn't nearly as hard as it had been several months ago. I thought it had something to do with taking the "esteemable actions" that Dr. Gerrie had discussed in the self-esteem seminar and that Isabel had also espoused.

"So, what's the lesson?" asked Edward rhetorically. "The lesson is that when you find things to be grateful about, you can laugh more. When you learn to appreciate yourself, you'll be more joyous."

Could I ever actually be joyous, I wondered? Then I smiled broadly at Edward.

⌒⌒

Edward gave us a homework assignment for the week between classes. He wanted us to look for as much humor in situations as possible and to think like stand-up comedians.

"Next week we're going to be very silly," and I want you to be prepared," he had told us.

I carried this thought into a meeting with the marketing people at work on Monday morning. The High Priestess of Marketing greeted us cordially, as she always did before sending an e-mail to my boss saying that she wanted revisions to my work.

"We've got some really exciting concepts to show you," said Beth, the senior creative in the meeting.

The High Priestess smiled weakly and typed in a URL on her computer. When our ad came up she stared at it in silence for several seconds. "I don't know why, but this seems sort of cartoony to me," she finally said.

"In what way do you mean?" asked Beth "Do you mean it's childish?"

The art director who had designed the ad bristled.

"No," said the High Priestess. "It's like a parody of an idea, but it's not an idea of a parody."

We all looked stumped.

Then the High Priestess scrolled down to see our second ad. "Now this I like," she said. We relaxed somewhat. "But there needs to be a stronger call to action. Something like, 'Redeem your free book pass now.'"

"How about, 'Redeem your free book pass now'"? I suggested.

"That is brilliant," said the High Priestess. She scrolled back up to the first ad. "This is sort of too *New Yorkery*," she said. Since I loved *The New Yorker*, it was now my turn to recoil.

"You mean you want something more serious?" asked Beth. "More *banky*."

"Yes, like it's on paper," said the High Priestess.

Clearly we had no idea what the woman was talking about and neither did she.

Minutes later I reflected on what had been funny about the meeting. At first, I couldn't think of anything. Then I started picturing the High Priestess's head on a donkey's body, with the caption "Big Marketing Jackass." That kind of tickled me.

Nothing funny happened the rest of the week, so I called my mother to see if anything funny had happened to her.

"One of my friends missed Mah-Jongg because she had to be taken to the hospital with chest pains," said my mother.

"What's so funny about that?" I asked.

"She was cheerful as ever," marveled my mother. "I'm thinking coronary bypass and she's laughing and telling me she'll see me next week in Mah-Jongg. Did you ever?"

Now I knew where I got my anticipatory anxiety from too.

At the next session, I expected Edward to go around the room and ask each of us to report on the funny things that had happened to us during the week. I felt reasonably certain that he would find neither of my stories particularly humorous. However, when I arrived for the class, Edward just wanted to know which of us had done our homework assignment of not reading, listening, or watching the news for a day.

"How did you feel?" Edward asked us. "Was it more work to not watch than to watch?"

"I had a terrible time," said the Texas lady. "Somebody e-mailed me a story by Jimmy Breslin and it was all I could do to delete it."

"How about you?" Edward asked the fibromyalgia woman, who looked like she was itching to participate.

"Well," she said, "it was tough—usually by the time my husband comes home I'm seething about something in the news. 'Did you hear this?' 'Did you hear that?' I ask him, and then I get down to phoning Washington and writing letters."

"Do you see how pervasive the news is and how it dominates our lives?" Edward asked.

"I don't know why they have some of those crazy shows on TV," the sculpture lady suddenly blurted. "I watch that Comedy Channel and I just don't find their ethnic humor very funny. I just don't get it."

"Of course everyone has a different sense of humor," said Edward. "I just bought this robot vacuum cleaner named Rumba and the way my cats run away from her is very funny to me."

I thought it was funny that Edward had called a machine "her," but decided that he could work that out in therapy. I also realized that everyone did have a different sense of humor, and the fact that some people didn't laugh at my jokes was not a reflection on me but said more about where they were coming from.

Next Edward led us through the same guided imagery exercise as he had in the previous class. "I want you to get away from that fast, shallow, stress breathing and take long, deep breaths," he said, "the kind of breaths that create beta brainwaves and increase your white blood cell count."

After that Edward asked us to imagine that we were back in the movie theater, smelling the popcorn and feeling the air conditioner, and then walking into the screen with scenes of laughter and joy in our lives.

The image I came up with was of getting stoned as a freshman in college, going to the laundry room and watching my clothes tumbling around in the dryer, as though they held the answer to some eternal mystery. The more I thought about it, the more I was transported back to that time and place.

When we were finished with the guided imagery, Edward asked if any of us wanted to share their joyous scenes with the class. The sculpture lady raised her hand and told us that when she was a child she and her friends used to put cardigans on backwards and put two oranges on their backs to simulate breasts. I couldn't see what could be so funny about that. It just seemed sort of, well, stupid, but this is a woman who had signed up for a sculpture course without an ounce of artistic talent.

"Does anyone else want to contribute his scene?" Edward asked when the sculpture lady was done. I desperately wanted to, but didn't know how my classmates would take the confession about my collegiate pot smoking. Before I had time to decide whether or not to raise my hand, Edward was talking about the history of humor research and telling us that in 1907 some brilliant social scientist had discovered that facial expressions could create emotional reactions.

"If you have a smile on your face, even a phony smile," Edward said, "it can create positive memories. Smiling makes us feel happy."

I can smile more.

"Now," Edward said, "I want you to get up and pretend that you are at a party full of people you don't know. I want you to walk around smiling at each other. No talking."

We all hesitantly got up.

"Go," said Edward.

We awkwardly milled around the room, briefly making eye contact and smiling at each other. There were a few people to whom I wanted to give whitening strips. I could only conjecture as to what they thought about my crooked teeth.

After thirty seconds, Edward called "time" and told us that he now wanted us to walk around and greet each other like we were long lost friends.

"Go," he said.

Immediately the Texas lady came up to me and gave me a bear hug. "It's so great to see you," she gushed.

"The feeling's mutual," I effused, wrapping my arms around her. I was quite proud of myself afterward, since public displays of affection had been outlawed in my family.

I sat down after the exercise and refocused. Edward was going on about the health benefits of smiling and laughter and introduced even more games for us to engage in. As we went through them, it occurred to me that they weren't very different from the ridiculous group therapy exercises I had to endure at the psychiatric hospital. This, in turn, reminded me of a psychiatric nurse in group who had pushed my leg off the arm of a chair and admonished me to sit like a lady.

When I came back to the class, Edward was urging us to form pairs. "Now you're going to tell your most intimate secrets to your partners, but you're to speak in no language recognized on earth."

I partnered with a Polish woman I hadn't noticed previously as Edward explained the exercise further. However, I wasn't really paying attention. I was back to thinking about the psychiatric hospital, about the night I had been admitted crying so hysterically that they had to give me a shot of sedative in my ass. And I thought about my initial roommate, a quiet Irish woman who told me that Jesus spoke to her. The next day, after ECT treatment, she hadn't even recognized me. And then there was the psychotic with the Mediterranean blue eyes who would stand just a few inches away and stare at me, unblinking, and the paranoid schizophrenic who thought my cigarette was bugged. Those people had been scary.

And that's when I realized that my time in the psychiatric hospital hadn't been all that great. Why had I believed otherwise? Then I had the most marvelous epiphany. It occurred to me that what I had been doing all along by remembering only the positive things about my hospitalization was an impressive bit of reframing—the very concept that Edward wanted us to retain above all else. I was actually getting an A in "Humor and Learned Optimism"! And by so doing, I had also closed Dr. Gerrie's Misery Gap quite considerably! I was filled with a sense of accomplishment.

Before I knew it, we had finished the gibberish game.

"For our next exercise, I'm going to need two volunteers," Edward said.

I raised my hand immediately.

Chapter 10

Up, Up and Away

I took my newfound confidence to work where I found that Todd, the grunting copywriter, had quit in a huff over money. The High Priestess of Marketing had decided that this was the perfect opportunity to speak to the vice president of creative operations about Todd's poor attitude.

"Why did they tell her this after he quit?" I asked my boss, Hugh. He just raised his hands as if to say, Who knows?

"All I *do* know," Hugh continued, "is that they are looking for another 'star' copywriter to replace him."

I sat across from Hugh feeling like a used Towelette. Then the words "I'm pretty decent" plopped out of my mouth.

"Oh, you're good. You're getting better every day. I didn't mean to … I didn't mean …" he fumbled.

The following day my supervisor apologized again. "Bill is always telling me that I say rude things without even knowing it," he said, referring to his partner.

"It's okay," I responded.

You see what a little moxie will get you, I thought. Getting what I wanted out of others without trampling on their feelings had always been the most difficult thing in the world for me. As a child, what I wanted more than anything was my parents' love, but I didn't know how to ask for it and didn't even know I had the right to ask for it, so I requested the only thing that was given in my family—material possessions. And I got them. But what I was interested in now, more than anything, was the ability to express my feelings in a way that would allow me to get what I really needed and wanted out of another human being. Hence, it was time for my biggest challenge yet—a class in assertiveness training.

As with my other classes, assertiveness training was filled with women. There were two men in the class—a college student who appeared to be suffering from a severe hangover and had his head down on his desk, and a tall, rugged man in his forties who was dressed in flannel and denim and reminded me of a lumberjack. Sitting in front of me was a lady in a pink sweater whose underwear I could see every time she leaned forward.

We were all seated impassively when suddenly a woman next to the wall cried out, "I've lost my screw!"

Subsequently half the class combed the floor for a part of the woman's eyeglasses. Into this walked our instructor, Fern Field, a woman who had very big brown hair and appeared to be composed of plastic from the boobs up. Taking command, Fern told all the women on the floor to get up because the classroom was too small and we had to move to a bigger one next door. The eyeglass woman reluctantly gave up her search.

Once we were in the new room, Fern took documents out of a big black tote and spread them across her desk. She placed about ten copies of her book at the front of the desk with a sign that gave the price as $19.95. Then she opened a bag of cookies and placed them on a table to the side.

"Life is uncertain," she said, "so eat dessert first."

There were a few snickers.

Fern told us that she was a practicing psychotherapist who dealt mostly with high achievers. She gave a lengthy laundry list of her achievements and handed out packets with a quote that read, "Your ability to influence people, personalities and behavior is a must."

"Just so you know," Fern explained, "I was your "sit in the back of the room and try to disappear into the wall" type of person. I was married and had the 2.5 kids like you were supposed to, and one day I saw an ad in a magazine for an assertiveness training program in California. I told my husband I was going."

I noticed that Fern was not wearing a wedding band and had probably thrown her husband out along with her passive behavior.

Fern went on to tell us that a famous philosopher (she wouldn't name names) had once said that we forfeit three fourths of ourselves to be liked by other people.

"This course is not about hooray for me and to hell with you. It's about getting your needs met without hurting other people."

"How do you deal with difficult bosses at work?" the eyeglass lady piped up.

"Just picture them going to the bathroom," Fern said.

She then embarked on a discussion of how people are eighty percent emotional and twenty percent logical.

"Even your authority figures are all little children inside," she stated. "They have all the same 'stuff' we have."

Fern told us that this was a course in helping people reach their potential. She read us the descriptions of three children who had been physically and emotionally abused and/or considered intellectually handicapped. She then told us that she was talking about Eleanor Roosevelt, Albert Einstein and Thomas Edison.

"You see?" said Fern. "When you see people's limits, they become limited."

In order to effect change, Fern told us that we had to have a positive attitude at all times and be persistent. While I wondered whether Edward had spoken to Fern about me and how brilliantly I had done in his class, our instructor launched into a protracted story about how she was able to extract a free round-trip ticket from

TWA. She proudly told us that she had done it by going though everyone in the chain of command until she got satisfaction out of the vice president of customer service in the airline's corporate office. At the end of the story, she proclaimed that people are like slot machines and that you have to keep going back to them until they cough up what you're after.

I thought about how I had been able to present my case to Hugh at work until he acknowledged my contributions.

Next Fern brandished a piece of chalk and drew on the blackboard a large circle that she divided into fifths.

"We're going to talk about different behavioral styles now," she said.

In one section, Fern wrote "DA" and told us that this style, *direct assertion*, involved direct, clear, brief and persuasive statements with no listening.

"This is like when you tell a telemarketer, 'I'm not interested.'"

Fern then went to another section and wrote "AR" for *ask and receive*.

"This is when you seek information and resources from others," she explained. "You need to show empathy and involvement and reinforce the positive. You need to listen and to summarize what's been said, as well as ask open-ended questions like, 'How do you feel about this?'"

At this point, Fern asked us to write down an ask-and-receive statement.

I thought of writing, "Please eat shit and die," but then I realized that this was a direct assertion statement and instead wrote, "So you're feeling like I don't listen to you."

I raised my hand to share my statement, but Fern picked on a pale young girl in her twenties wearing a floral print shirt and glaring oval-shaped glasses with black frames.

"I'm the youngest in my office," she stated, "and I feel uncomfortable telling all these people in their forties what to do."

"In my book, which is available here for the low price of $19.95," said Fern, "I say not to think of people as lazy or to make judgments about them. Instead, try to catch them doing almost the right thing."

The floral girl looked perplexed, so Fern gave an example of a person working on one task while letting another, more imperative job slide.

"You could say something like, 'I really appreciate all the work you've done on *A*, but *B* still needs to get done.'"

The floral girl seemed momentarily satisfied. Then Fern blurted out, "Some adults you find in the workplace are like special ed children."

While we were digesting the comment, our instructor was already on a jag about not allowing yourself to be victimized. She said the worst audiences were teachers and singles because neither could manage to shut up while she was talking. She told us about a particular instance in which she was talking to a group of singles and someone raised her hand and said, "It's people like you who are responsible for divorce in this world."

"So I said, 'That is a very good point and we're going to address that,'" Fern told us.

"Did you ever address it?" I asked, slightly stung because I was single.

"No, but I shut her up," Fern remarked.

The floral girl raised her hand again and Fern nodded in her direction.

"What about office gossips?" she asked. "Everyone in my office gossips about this Holocaust survivor and I started yelling at them."

"Let it go," said Fern. "It's just a part of human nature."

"But what if it's work-related gossip," the floral girl pressed. "And what if the person gossiping has the ear of management?"

"Well," said Fern, completely avoiding the question, "you need to not personalize it. We all have expectations and disappointments. That's life. It's unfair."

The floral girl looked very dissatisfied, but Fern wasn't paying attention; she was filling in another section of the pie and labeling it "AT" for *assert together*.

"Now, say your spouse wants to go on a ski vacation and you want to go on a beach vacation. What do you do?"

"You get a divorce," I offered. There was a smattering of laughter.

"No," said Fern, without cracking a smile. "This calls for a style of behavior that requires brainstorming together and engaging in problem solving and conflict resolution. Facts, opinions, thoughts and feelings are shared, and each person asks questions, summarizes and listens. Remember, 'listen' uses the same letters as 'silent.'"

Fern waited for us to be openly appreciative of her profundity, but we weren't, so she decided to ask us for possible solutions to this particular conflict.

"What about if you say, 'Go on your goddamn ski vacation, but don't expect sex any time soon,'" I joked. A burst of laughter erupted from the left side of the room.

"No, I don't think that would work," said Fern sourly.

"Then how about telling your husband you'd like to compromise and go on a vacation that you can both enjoy, like Europe," I said. "Or that you'd like to go to a place like California that has skiing and the beach."

"Those are both great suggestions," said Fern.

"If married couples actually did this, there would be a lot less divorce," said the lumberjack somberly.

At this point, I felt compelled to respond. "Married couples can do this," I said. "I've seen it." And I had. My sickly brother had wound up with a wonderfully communicative wife, and they had open lines of discourse.

"Married couples can do it in Utopia," scoffed the lumberjack. I made a note to call his wife at our next break and urge counseling.

In the meantime, Fern filled up another section of the pie with the letters "AG" and told us that this stood for *aggressive*.

"This is negative, judgmental, angry, blaming, sarcastic," she said. *Now we're getting into familiar territory.*

Next Fern wrote "NA" for *non-assertive*. "This is blaming others, being apologetic, whining, people pleasing and approvalseeking."

Wow, I thought, even more familiar.

"Say you're in a restaurant and you order a steak well done," Fern went on, "and you get a steak that is rare. An aggressive person would say to the waiter, 'With a little CPR you could bring this meat back to life,' while the non-assertive person would say, 'The steak's fine.'"

I recognized the latter one as my typical approach.

"But," Fern continued, "you could say, 'This steak is a little rare, but with a little more fire under it, I'm sure it will taste fine.'"

I turned this over in my mind and came to the conclusion that in my glory days, I would sooner have gone back and cooked the steak myself. Perhaps I don't have to do that anymore, I thought.

While I mulled this over, Fern became philosophical. "I believe all our problems would be over if we just said 'yes' more of the time," she said.

"But you don't want to be a pushover," I noted.

"Of course," said Fern, looking annoyed, but I didn't mind. Who was she but just another psychobabbler?

"Everything that happens to us happens when it is supposed to happen," proclaimed Fern. "There are no mistakes, only different outcomes."

"So, whatever happens, happens for the best?" asked the lumberjack.

"Exactly," said Fern.

"I don't believe that," said the lumberjack.

What a downer, I thought. Is that the way I had sounded? I didn't want to wait for the break. I wanted to call the lumberjack's wife immediately and find out if she was busy packing her suitcases, but Fern moved on and I felt like I simply had to keep up.

"You have to stay positive even if you are in a negative situation," she said. "If you're around a negative person, don't buy into the doom and gloom."

"Just walk away," said the floral girl as I looked around the room to see if anyone was staring at me. But why would they be? I'd done nothing to draw attention.

"Or change the subject," said Fern.

"You feel so tired with those people," said the floral girl.

"We all know drama queens," said Fern. "Those people who go to the dry cleaners, and what happens there is a big deal."

I remembered an incident at my dry cleaners about a year ago. I had found that a coat I dropped off still had a spot on it. I complained about this bitterly for days and asked everyone I spoke to for advice on whether to switch dry cleaners. I couldn't possibly still be like that, I thought.

Now Fern told us to "pay with praise" and not to "overinstruct."

"My father overinstructed," said Fern in her sole brush with bitterness. He asked me to paint and then gave me hundreds of directions to the point where I gave him back the paintbrush."

Clearly, I thought, Fern was yet another individual who had issues with her parents.

"But what if it comes out screwed up?" asked the lumberjack.

"How do you mean?" asked Fern

"Well, I asked my wife to paint the radiator and she went ahead and did it with one of those small tester brushes. It took days."

"People are different. You just have to leave her alone to do it her way."

"But then she didn't make me dinner for two days," cried the lumberjack.

There was a spontaneous roar of outrage from all the women in the class, at which point the lumberjack bowed his head in shame, and I wondered how many married men were sitting at home thinking evil thoughts about their wives. It occurred to me that marriage did not equal eternal bliss, and that perhaps I should look for the good things about—or *reframe*—being single.

"Perhaps you can communicate your feelings to your wife," Fern said.

"Perhaps," said the lumberjack.

A few of the older women in the class exchanged looks and shook their heads. They knew.

After a brief break, Fern told us that we were now going to engage in role-playing. She explained that she was going to give us statements and that after each one we'd have to decide whether it was a DA or AR situation and respond with the "soft assertion" listed in our packets. I looked at my list of soft assertions. I saw terms like "appreciation," "approval," "assurance" and "affection." I thought of the people in my group from Humor and Learned Optimism and remembered that I had expressed all of these things to them.

"All right," Fern said, "the first situation is that you're in a restaurant and are led over to a seat near a table of children. Write down what you are going to say to the waiter."

I thought for a moment and then wrote as a joke, "Why the hell did you put me at this table? Get me out of here." Then I wrote, "direct assertion."

"Next," said Fern, "a negative person keeps complaining to you. What do you say to him?"

I wrote down, "Will you please shut the fuck up." After that I wrote, "direct assertion."

Fern led us through about ten more situations ranging from "You've been promoted to supervisor, but your staff still sees you as a peer and doesn't listen" to "Your friend or spouse is pouting lately because you're spending more time on interests of your own."

I swiftly wrote down my comic answers and placed a "DA" after each one.

"Now," said Fern, when we were all finished, "I want you to pick a partner and go through all your answers and what style of expression you chose."

I looked over and noticed a young woman in her twenties sitting just to my left. She had on red Adidas sweat pants with white piping and white sneakers with red shoelaces.

"Hi," I said to her. "I'm Wendy."

"I'm Beatrice," she said with an accent.

"Where are you from?" I asked her.

"Brazil," she told me.

What is it with these foreigners and me?

"Do you work?" I asked her.

"No, I'm taking this class for college credit. I'm majoring in hotel management."

"Oh, that's great," I said. "Can you get me a free room at the Ritz Carlton in Laguna Niguel?

"What?" she said.

"Never mind," I said. It was clear that I was wasting my sense of humor on Beatrice, but I was determined not to back down. "What did you put for the first answer?"

"I wrote, 'I really love this restaurant but would appreciate it if you could seat me at another table.'"

"That's pretty good," I said. Then I read my response.

"You can't say that!" yelled Beatrice.

"Yes, I can!" I yelled back. "I wrote down that it was a DA for direct assertion.

"It's aggressive," said Beatrice.

"I realize you feel it's aggressive, but I don't," I said.

"We're supposed to be assertive!" Beatrice countered.

"I was just joking around!" I finally yelled back.

"Oh," said Beatrice, suddenly somewhat subdued. "Still, it's a good thing you took this class."

I have an AG for you, I wanted to say. Go take a high dive into the shallow end of a pool.

After everyone was done, Fern announced that everything we say to people either erodes or builds up our self-esteem. At this juncture, I gave Beatrice a dirty glance for trying to erode my self-esteem. Fern then proceeded to go over each item and identify appropriate assertive responses. As most of Beatrice's responses were similar, she cast a superior eye in my direction. It didn't bother me. I knew that had I answered seriously, I would have come up with the same responses.

"Even with difficult people we have to develop a rapport before we communicate with them," Fern said. "When I go into a department store, I always smile and say hello to the salespeople, even though the clerks in New York are terribly rude."

Fern digressed for a moment and told us how cheerful everyone in the rest of the country was and then wrote on the blackboard like a madwoman.

After she was done with her scribbling, our instructor told us that there were different expressions of assertiveness ranging from expressing wants and needs to instances where empathy is called for and where preventive measures had to be taken.

"You're going to meet resistance," Fern stated firmly. "You'll get silence, anger, avoidance, criticism and feigned illness."

"I feel nauseous," I whispered to Beatrice, who promptly gave me a dirty look.

Fern went on to tell us that we were going to engage in another role-playing exercise with our partners. She told us that one of us would be the employer and one would be the employee, and that the former was trying to get the latter to learn a new system but was meeting resistance.

"Who do you want to be?" I asked Beatrice.

"I'll be the employee," she said.

"All right, then. I have to convince you to use the new system."

"No," said Beatrice. "I have to convince you."

"No," I responded. "Why would the employee need to convince the employer of something like that?" Beatrice looked like she was thinking about the problem in her native Portuguese tongue. I was getting impatient and felt that I was in imminent danger of becoming aggressive, when Beatrice caved in to my way of thinking and said she would be the employer.

"Fine," I said. "I'll be the employee. Go ahead."

"Wendy, I have this new system that I would really like you to start using," said Beatrice.

"No," I said, crossing my arms. "Ed in accounting didn't have to learn it, so I don't see why I should have to."

"Ed is going to learn the new system," Beatrice continued.

"When?" I sniped. I had decided that I was going to make things very difficult for Beatrice.

"Tomorrow," she said.

"I don't think it's a good idea. I'm getting my work done well the way things are."

"But this will make your job easier to do. You'll get done sooner," implored Beatrice.

"Will I get done by two p.m.?" I asked.

"Yes," said Beatrice.

"Then I'll be able to get off work at two p.m.?" I asked.

"Yes," said Beatrice.

"And if I'm learning a new skill, will I be compensated for it financially?" I asked Beatrice.

"Okay," said Beatrice.

"And will I also get to bring my cat to work?" I asked.

"*Cagao*," said Beatrice.

"What does that mean?" I asked.

"It means *shit* in Portuguese," said Beatrice.

"That's aggressive," I said.

"But you're impossible," said Beatrice.

Before we could get into a full-blown argument, Fern stopped the class and asked us how the exercise had gone. I hadn't heard any voices raised, so I surmised that Beatrice and I were the only ones who had almost come to blows. Now Fern was back at the chalkboard scribbling all the conditions for good listening.

"You must want to listen," she told us. "You have to stop yourself from expressing or defending. Also, don't interrupt with 'yes, buts'— you have to keep your *but* out of the way."

"I'm the queen of *buts*," said Beatrice, trying to make amends.

I tried to smile, but couldn't.

"You have to decode the messages and find out what the person really means by what they are saying," Fern went on. Then she gave us the statement, "We wouldn't have missed the sign if you weren't talking."

What is he really saying?" Fern asked us.

"He's saying that he's worried that they're lost and won't get there in time," I said when called upon.

"Exactly," said Fern, who then gave us the statement, "'This store is impossible. All the salespeople are incompetent.' Now after decoding, what would you say to such a customer?" Fern asked.

Kiss my ass in Macy's window? I wanted to offer, but before I could, the pink lady volunteered, "What can I do to help you?"

"Perfect," said Fern.

As we progressed through the statements, I was heartened to find that my decoding skills were ample when I really put my mind to it. It definitely took more effort, but I could see that it would be worth it. Fern next told us that we were to engage in a group exercise. We would read about a situation in our packet and then see all the possible responses to it, determining which behavioral styles applied and selecting the best and the worst response. "There has to be unanimous agreement in the group," explained Fern. "If you don't like one person's answer, you can't just say, 'Shut up and pick my answer.'"

As the groups coalesced, I decided that it would probably be best if Beatrice and I were not together. I looked in another direction and suddenly fell in with the lumberjack and floral girl and a few others. Well, it wasn't perfect, but it would have to do. Before we got started, Fern advised us to turn to the page in our packet on assertive goals and mark down a few things we hoped to achieve. I marked off "talk more" because I figured the people at work would appreciate that, and "be expressive," "be empathic" and "be persistent."

A few minutes later, we got underway. The first situation had to do with a salesman who had been calling on a company for well over a year seeking business, but had been rebuffed even though he had the product that the company needed at a price that was right. "In your most recent sales call, you pressed a little more, pointing out the benefits of using your product and the reliability of your company. The customer responded by saying, 'Look, we're just starting a run and I'm very busy this week. Let me think about it, and maybe next time you come here I'll give you an order.' You respond by saying …"

Beneath the situation were the responses, which consisted of the following:

Response A: As you know I have been calling on you for a year now and you have put me off quite a few times. Each time it has been a different excuse. I think the reasonable thing to do is to give me the order now. After all, I'm a professional in this business. I know what you need and it's about time we got something going.

Response B: OK. That's great. Actually, I'd like to get you started now. Frankly, I know that when you start using our product, it is going to become increasingly evident that it has the quality you need. I can deliver 100 cartons this month, then when I make my next call, we can take a really close look at how the product worked out for you and we will have a sound basis for looking at your needs in the future.

Response C: What information do you need to help you make up your mind today?

Response D: I'm sorry to have to press you but I'm getting a lot of flack from my boss to get your company to use our product. Why not take a small order this week—you'll make me look good and you'll find our product meets your needs.

After I read all the responses, I put down my answers, stating that response A was the worst response and response C the best response. I felt reasonably sure of my choices and was ready to boldly defend my honor in an assertive, not aggressive, way.

"What did everyone put for response A?" said the floral girl taking control of the group. We all agreed that response A was aggressive.

Relieved, I told everyone that I had interpreted response B to be a direct assertion.

The floral girl looked at me disapprovingly. "I put aggressive for that one too" she said bluntly. Then the lumberjack said, "I put ask and receive for that one."

"But how is it AR?" the floral girl asked.

"They're going to work it out together on the next order," said the lumberjack.

"No, they're not," said the floral girl. "He's just telling the company what he's going to do. He's not offering any options."

"But there's a discussion going on," tried the lumberjack.

"There's no discussion," said the floral girl, getting animated. "What if the client is a dentist and the salesman tells him he's going to send him one hundred toothbrushes, but then the dentist drops dead and so he doesn't need one hundred toothbrushes?"

"Boy, do you have a vivid imagination," said the lumberjack.

At this point, the floral girl went back to her notes and restated all the conditions for an AR behavioral style. "There is no listening and summarizing," she spat at the lumberjack. "There are no open-ended questions. There's no empathy."

"But I can see where he's coming from," I said, at this point actually starting to feel sorry for the lumberjack.

The argument went on for several more minutes and was followed by more rancorous debates over which response meant what. By the time we got to the third situation, which also revolved around work, barely anyone in our group was talking.

A few minutes later, Fern called "time" and the discussion came to an end. She proceeded to go over all the answers and tell us which ones were correct. This caused further consternation and debate, not to mention that every time the floral girl's position was proven right, she smirked at us.

"This all depends on how it's stated," I said at one point during the continuing debate over direct assertion and ask and receive.

"That is a most excellent point," said Fern. "It's all a question of perception."

Fern then launched into a story about how she was having a hamburger at a McDonald's once when a group of "rowdy teens" came over, picked up her pocketbook and proceeded to walk out of the restaurant with it. "It didn't even occur to me that this was a robbery," said Fern proudly, "so jovially I said to the kid, 'Quit your kidding around and give me back my pocketbook.' He was so shocked by my attitude that he returned the bag and ran out of the place."

There was a long moment of silence as we contemplated what a loon Fern was and how easily she could have been killed.

"Now I'm going to tell you how to get difficult people onboard," she said, hurriedly changing the subject. She then offered a detailed list about the types we were likely to encounter in a work environment and tips on getting around them. Fortunately I couldn't recognize any of my co-workers in her descriptions of the defiant, the angry, the argumentative, the helpless, the critical, the sullen and the many more land mines in the office landscape.

Fern wanted to close our session with a little guided imagery because, she said, "this is what all the gurus do."

She told us to close our eyes and turned on some uplifting music.

"I want you to imagine that you are sitting in a luxurious hot tub with the bubbles caressing your skin," said Fern in a soothing voice. "Your arms and legs feel warm and heavy. Your breathing is relaxed. No matter what happens, you are going to remain calm. You find that you are respected in the workplace for your intelligence, your skills and your ingenuity. You find you have an incredible amount of energy and enthusiasm for your job. You find great joy using your new assertiveness skills …"

The interesting thing was, I could actually picture myself in this situation.

After babbling for a few more minutes, Fern brought us back. "How does everyone feel?" she asked.

"Are you available for personal consultations?" asked the lumberjack. "I don't know what to do about my wife."

"Take my card," said Fern. "I always have time."

"Yeah, but do you have a lifetime?" asked the lumberjack.

And that's when I definitively decided that at times I was grateful I was single.

When I got home, I checked my e-mail and noted that I had a missive from my overseas agent, telling me that he was sending my manuscript out to another "contact." He never told me who these contacts were exactly, and in the year that we had been together, I had received only two rejections from editors to whom he had sent my book. I decided that he was not doing enough for me and that I needed a change.

I could have sent my agent an e-mail relieving him of his services, but I decided that would be too wimpish. This was the perfect opportunity to put to work what I had just learned in my class, I reasoned. I got his phone number off his Web site and dialed. "Authors First," a British voice said on the other side. There was a slight echo and he did, indeed, sound an ocean away.

"James?" I said.

"Yes?"

"It's Wendy Aron from New York."

"Wendy! So good to hear from you! How are you?"

"I'm good. How are you?"

"Good. Good," he said.

"James, I wish I had something cheerier to say, but I've been giving it a lot of thought and I really feel that it's not working out with us and that I need to find another agent."

"What are you talking about?" said James. "I'm just getting started."

"James, I understand how you can feel that you have more to give, but I'm unhappy with the lack of response, and I feel I could be better serviced by an agent in the United States."

"It takes time to get responses," said James.

"I understand how difficult it is, but I'm just not satisfied," I replied.

"Just give me one more shot," said James. "I've just been in touch with another editor in New York."

"I'm afraid I've made up my mind," I said.

"I'm sorry you feel that way," said James.

"I'm sorry too," I said. "I appreciate your faith in me."

"Good luck," said James. Then I heard a click on the other end.

Ask and receive, I said to myself. And then I gave myself an A-plus in assertiveness training.

Chapter 11

Ms. Happiness

"Do you have any interest in going to an air show?" my friend Elaine asked me one day. I remembered my pledge to do more adventurous things with Elaine, but I was hesitant.

"Is that like where you see on the news a plane crashes and kills the pilot and several innocent spectators?" I asked.

"That's actually only happened a few times," said Elaine. "And it mostly happens overseas."

Somewhat placated, I agreed to meet Elaine at a supermarket near where she lived and have her drive the rest of the way to the show. The last time we had met at this location, I had witnessed a major domestic squabble in the parking lot wherein a woman in a large SUV had blocked her apparent ex-husband from pulling out in his car until he agreed to pay child support. Much to my disappointment, Elaine had whisked me away before there was actually any violence.

On this particular afternoon, it took me about an hour to get to the lot, and once there I noticed that things were pretty calm.

"Can't we wait to see if any little family dramas develop?" I asked Elaine.

"Get in the car," said Elaine sternly.

I piled in with my road trip essentials—Jell-O fruit snacks and bottled water. A few minutes into our journey, Elaine asked me if I had heard about the "incident" at an air show in Indiana the previous week.

"What incident?" I asked, getting a little nervous.

"Never mind," said Elaine. "Isn't it a perfect day?"

The tires of her car screeched as she tore onto a two-lane highway.

"It's okay," I said.

"Now this turns into a one-lane road a few miles up, so we might get a little backed up there," Elaine mentioned. Two minutes later we were in bumper-to-bumper traffic going absolutely nowhere.

"Oh, well. What are you going to do?" said Elaine.

A half hour later we had moved approximately one hundred yards and Elaine said something like, "If I get out of here and head east and then head west and then south and then north we should get ahead of this car in front of us."

I loved Elaine's optimism. "Go for it," I said.

I hadn't slept well the night before and was starting to feel tired, so I told my friend that the fact that I was going to close my eyes didn't mean I was bored by her company.

"Don't you want to see where I grew up?" Elaine asked, sounding a little put off.

I agreed to keep my eyes open for a few more minutes. This was the only signal Elaine needed to embark on a cheerful discourse about the different homes she had lived in as a child. There were a lot of them, and apparently they each merited detailed descriptions.

"I'm closing my eyes NOW," I finally said. Elaine promptly shut up. I wasn't able to nap so I opened my eyes about fifteen minutes later.

"It didn't feel like we were moving," I said in a haze.

"We weren't," said Elaine, the picture of serenity. "We've been sitting here."

"Oh, great," I said.

"Want a Tootsie Pop?" Elaine asked, withdrawing the candy from her handbag.

"Maybe we should just call it a day," I said.

"Oh, no," said Elaine. "We'll get there."

We wound up sitting in the car in traffic for the next hour and a half. All told, it took us two hours to travel fifteen miles. When we finally got to the closed aerospace facility and airfield where the event was to take place, we were directed to an open grass field to park. The terrain was rough and we bumped around in the car.

"I feel like I'm going to throw up," I said.

"Hang on. We're almost there!" trilled Elaine, pulling into a spot that I knew we would never be able to locate again.

"And I have to pee!" I stated forcefully.

"All right, all right," said Elaine. "We'll get you taken care of."

Elaine popped the trunk and took out a camera, camcorder, two folding chairs and a pair of binoculars.

"Where do we have to go?" I whined, noticing a steady stream of people filtering into an area that looked like it was a mile away. Elaine nodded her head in their direction.

"We have to walk all the way there?" I complained.

"Calm down," said Elaine. "I'll carry most of the stuff."

With that, she trudged off in the direction of the crowd of people, carrying most of her belongings.

"I have to pee!" I insisted, tripping over the weeds in the grassy field we were traversing. I realized that not having had my needs met as a child had made me a very demanding adult.

"All right!" Elaine screamed.

About half a mile later, sweating profusely, we arrived at a large tarmac where hundreds of parents and their kids had congregated, their heads turned skywards as they sat in beach chairs.

"Look, there's the bathroom," said Elaine, pointing to a row of green portable toilets off to the side. I ran toward them.

"Oh, my God," I said as we approached. "Will you look at this."

There in front of us was a line of what must have been over one hundred people waiting to relieve themselves.

"I'll bet it moves fast," said Elaine.

"I wouldn't count on it," I rejoined.

When I finally got into a bathroom, I realized that it was nothing more than a hole surrounded by plastic, filled with human excrement and used toilet paper. I tried to pull down my jeans and underwear, but I was so sweaty they stuck to my skin. With great difficulty, I was finally able to get my garments off. After I peed, I was desperate to wash my hands of my filthy surroundings, but there were no sinks in the toilet. In fact there was no plumbing of any sort.

"Jews aren't cut out for places like this," I told Elaine upon exiting.

"I didn't see any signs that said 'No Jews allowed,' " my friend said.

"Oh, we don't need signs," I said. "We know."

Elaine and I soon found a patch of grass to situate our folding chairs. Families consisting of irritated parents desperately waiting for something to happen that would shut their kids up surrounded us. The children screamed. They wanted to go to the carnival set up a few hundred yards to our right. They wanted to go to the bathroom. They wanted to tour the inside of a FedEx plane on the tarmac.

"Isn't this fun?" Elaine said.

"I didn't know you hated me this much," I said.

Shortly, a small blue and yellow plane, which our program described as a PT 17 Stearman, streaked by. The plane climbed straight up, seemed to dangle in the air and then plunged down, twisting like a corkscrew before it pulled out of its descent perilously close to the runway.

"What the hell was that?" I asked Elaine.

"Haven't you ever seen an air show on television?" my friend snorted.

"Well excuse me," I said. "I just don't understand how anyone from the same species as me could do such a thing. My idea of risk taking is crossing while the street sign flashes 'Don't Walk.'"

"If you read the program, you'd see that they are all third- and fourth-generation pilots," said Elaine condescendingly. "This kind of thing is in their blood."

"Well, bully for them," I said.

While Elaine watched the pilots of a bunch of other airplanes with nicknames like Warthog and Thunderbolt defy sanity, I focused on the family sitting just in front of us. The husband, in a tight blue tank top, blue jeans and construction boots, was lithe and muscular. The wife was shaped like Humpty Dumpty and wore thin, tight white cotton shorts through which one could easily see her underwear. The kids, a boy and a girl, looked like neither of them. How had this couple met? At a bar or a bowling alley most likely. Had she been thin when they met? Was he sneaking off to topless bars to bang waitresses of poor white trash stock? I was always curious about other people and their stories. I noted that I had met and heard a lot of them in the past year.

"Isn't this great?" Elaine asked. She was standing and capturing the air show on her camcorder.

"Are you going to sell the tape to CNN when one of the planes crashes?" I asked.

"Only if it's not a fatal crash," she said. "I don't want to make money off someone's death."

"How sporting of you," I said. "Is it time to go yet?"

"We just got here," said Elaine, her voice rising. At this moment we were overcome by the overwhelming smell of human waste.

"They must be cleaning the portable toilets," Elaine said cheerfully.

"Now the smell will go away."

"It doesn't take much to make you happy," I said.

"Are you really having that terrible a time?" she asked me.

"No," I said. "I get some of my greatest pleasure out of complaining to you when you drag me places."

When I got home that night, I thought about what I had really liked most about my friend Elaine, and I arrived at the conclusion that it was her joy for life. Then a bubble popped into my head filled with all of the instructors, gurus, consultants, classmates and friends I had spoken to over the past year. They all screamed in unison, "You can be full of joy, too, if you only let yourself be."

But where had all these people found their happiness? No sooner had I realized that I was still searching for a state of "invulnerable euphoria" than I signed up for a continuing education class with Jane Mayer, a woman who was semi-famous because she had an in-law who had been a regular on *Saturday Night Live*. Jane was known on the country club circuit as "Ms. Happiness" because she had apparently suffered many tragedies and had managed to retain a positive attitude despite them. She now went around the country lecturing on how to do the same.

"You're going to love her," gushed my star-struck sister-in-law when I told her I was going to see Jane. "She's got so much energy."

When I arrived at the meeting room where the seminar was to be held, I immediately became aware of what my sister-in-law had been talking about. Jane, a large, dynamic woman dressed in black and wearing a gold necklace the size of a Clydesdale's yoke, held court with several members of the audience whom she apparently knew.

"Oh, he went to school with my ex-cousin's third wife," she said to one participant. Then to another, "My friend asked me why I was talking to her, since we weren't on speaking terms, but I couldn't even remember what we were fighting about."

Once the room became packed, again mostly with women, Jane got underway.

"Most of you are here because you heard I have a famous relative, right?" she asked. "Well, I'll tell you a story about that."

Jane then proceeded to tell a tale about how she had met Barbra Streisand through her famous relative and had actually played poker with the über-celebrity.

"I looked up and there was Donna Karan on one side and Barbra on the other," she said. "It was the perfect moment."

After the story, Jane gestured to an easel and pad beside her that said, "How to Be Happy."

"That is the silliest title for a class I have ever heard," she said. "I don't think anyone can tell you how to be happy, but I can tell you my story."

She went on to relate that when she was eight, her father had been killed in a traffic accident, and that her mother didn't tell her what had happened to him until six years later. Her mother, meanwhile, suffered from treatment-resistant depression and was in and out of mental hospitals for years. Her aunt and uncle raised her, but both died before she turned eighteen. She got married at nineteen to a compulsive gambler. They had to declare bankruptcy. She got a divorce from him and the next day her son was killed in an auto collision. After that she became a housebound agoraphobic for eleven years.

After Jane had finished her story, the audience sat in stunned silence. "You may be thinking, 'How did she survive?'" Jane said. "You know what the answer is? Laughter."

Jane went on to tell us that some time after her son died, she turned to her daughter and said, "You may have lost a brother, but I lost a son who owed me tons of money. I'll never get that money back." Jane continued, "I heard a 'gigglet' from her, and I knew we were going to laugh again."

"But that's just you," someone from the audience yelled out.

"It's a choice that everyone can make," Jane countered. "I decided to laugh and be happy. There was no map and it was a bumpy journey, but I didn't want to be in pain, so I chose a road filled with positive thoughts."

We must have continued to look skeptical because Jane then told us about how she had once met Deepak Chopra and asked him for words of wisdom. "You know what he said? He said, 'You are the dinka of your doughts.'" Translated, Jane told us that that meant, "You are the thinker of your thoughts."

"Whatever you decide to believe is what the reality is," she said. "You can choose a joyful or a sad life."

After several more stories about how she conquered loss, pain and grief through laughter, Jane asked us if anyone in the audience was depressed. Before I could raise my hand, an elderly woman in the front row did.

"Who makes you laugh?" Jane asked her.

"I have a happy side and a sad side," the woman said.

Jane looked like she was trying to figure out how this response could relate to her question. "Yes, but who makes you laugh?" she repeated.

"All my friends are dead, so I have to have to watch television," said the woman. "I watch reruns of *Seinfeld*. Sometimes that makes me laugh."

"Good, that's very good," Jane responded. "Now I want all of you to turn toward the person sitting next to you and smile."

I turned and smiled at a woman wearing the most obnoxious glasses I had ever seen. They were huge and had multicolored frames. Only in New York City.

"You see," Jane said, "when you get out of yourself and relate to another person, you instantly feel better."

This has been true for me, I thought. Witness my most recent excursion with Elaine.

"But how do you get out of the box?" another lady asked.

"You start by laughing," reiterated Jane.

"But it's hard if you're a serious person," said the woman.

"Just buy a video of someone who makes you laugh," Jane pressed.

"Nobody makes me laugh," said the woman.

"You start with a small step," said Jane. "In the early days, I would buy a fake nose and glasses and stand in front of the mirror telling myself how miserable I was. It cracked me up."

Why hadn't I thought of doing that? I wondered.

"You didn't tell us how you got out of bankruptcy," a man piped up.

"I lived on friends' couches," said Jane.

"I don't have any friends," said the man.

"You can always find a friend," Jane insisted. "You just ask for help."

"From who?" snorted the man. "From the government?"

"I'm just saying that none of us is alone," said Jane, trying to avoid a political discussion.

"What about the homeless?" the man stressed.

"The homeless made the choice to be homeless," stated Jane. "I was homeless and I promised myself that I would never be homeless again. I worked out of a shopping bag."

"That's you," said the man.

A few people voiced their agreement with the man and a number of other hands shot up.

"I read of a study that said we are all pre-programmed by our genes to be happy or unhappy, and our experiences and attitudes have very little to do with it," said a man. He must have read the same article I had about everyone having a certain baseline of happiness.

"That is not true," said Jane. "I was not a happy camper and I changed my outlook."

"This study was done at Harvard," said the man crisply.

"It all has to do with practice," said Jane. "You have to practice being joyful, just like you have to practice the piano if you want to play in a concert."

"I don't know if I agree with that," said the man.

"It all has to do with your comfort level," replied Jane. "If you're comfortable being miserable, that's where you'll go."

"But there are some things you can't change," said a thirtyish man in the back of the room.

"Like what?" asked Jane, walking toward him.

"Like if you're a C student you can't become an A student."

"But you can be the best C student there is," said Jane, positively glowing.

The man seemed to shrug her off as more and more depressed people raised their hands to challenge Jane's assertions about happiness.

"Do you know what I do on days I see the sunrise?" asked Jane rhetorically. "I thank God for the glorious day that is sure to be."

"Are there any words you repeat to convince yourself of this?" asked a hopeful woman.

"You have to eliminate 'I can't' and replace it with 'I will,'" said Jane.

My classmates slumped in their chairs, defeated. And that's when I decided that if the last year had taught me anything, it was that most people were not happy most of the time.

Chapter 12

The New Plan

I don't know what it was that made me go to the Depression Support Group sponsored by a local hospital—perhaps it was Isabel's advice to go places where I belonged—but one October evening I drove over to the off-site medical office building where it was held. As I sat down in the crowded reception area where all the visitors congregated, a very commanding blonde woman in a leopard print leotard marched in and announced to the receptionist that we were all present for the depression meeting and wanted to go back to the room.

"You can't go back. It's not time yet," said the receptionist sternly.

"You're kidding," said the blonde woman. "It's three minutes to eight."

The receptionist shook her head.

"What's the matter, Jean?" asked a man wearing cowboy boots.

"They won't let us in," said the woman, clearly exasperated. "They probably think we'll break the furniture."

The leopard woman took a seat. A few more minutes passed and she got up and walked over to the receptionist. "I have eight," she said, tapping her wristwatch. "Can we go in?"

"You need a therapist with you."

"Well, the therapist is late," fumed the leopard woman.

"Jean, they are going to have to sedate you," quipped the man in cowboy boots.

"Oh, there he is," said the leopard woman, pointing to a smug looking man in his thirties who gestured for us to follow him to the meeting room.

"They think we need supervision," huffed Jean as we walked down the hallway.

Suddenly, the institutional odor I remembered from my days in the bin permeated the air. I recalled having to line up while the psychiatric nurses condescendingly handed out our medications, much like Nurse Ratched in *One Flew Over the Cuckoo's Nest*. Now I saw that the smug looking man was staring at me with the look of possibility in his eye. Then, almost instantly, he seemed to remind himself that I was not dating material because I was one of the nuts. I didn't like being placed in that category.

A short time later I found myself in a "rap" group of about eight other sufferers. Eric, the depressive facilitator, urged us to share as much as we cared to about our circumstances. He began by saying that he was experiencing a setback and had gone on Social Security disability and was no longer working.

"It's important to note that setbacks are not permanent," said the leopard woman. "And no one should feel like a failure for having a setback."

It was the first truly genuine thing I had heard in some time because it didn't come attached to a class or consultation fee.

Next a handsome man in his early thirties explained how he had been hospitalized six times in the past two years and had had three different psychiatrists, each of whom diagnosed him with something different and placed him on a different medication.

"Sometimes they can do more harm than good," said the leopard woman. She is so right, I thought, reflecting on the psychiatrist I had seen in Los Angeles.

Soon a very heavy woman in a blue T-shirt spoke. She had a very short neck and her head seemed to rest on her shoulders. "I haven't been feeling too well lately," said the woman, her voice cracking. "In June I tried to … I tried to kill myself, but they found me."

"Did you really want to die?" asked Eric.

"A part of me did, but I made sure I did it near Hamilton Hill just in case I lived."

"Hamilton Hill?" said the leopard woman.

"It's the hospital where Billy Joel detoxed. It's a very good hospital."

"And what have you been doing since then?" one of the women in the group inquired gingerly.

"I went back to my job," said the woman.

"So, they were supportive at your job?" asked Eric.

"Not at all," said Hamilton Hill. "I called one of my co-workers before I did it and told her that I was going to kill myself."

"Did she try to get you help?" asked Eric.

"No, she reported me, because there's a company policy against threatening to harm yourself. I was reprimanded."

Jeez, that is real craziness, I thought.

"That's some company," said the leopard lady.

"They send jokes about me and Billy Joel in the interoffice e-mail," said Hamilton Hill. "I've seen them."

"Can you get a new job?" I asked.

Hamilton Hill's eyes got misty. "What do I say when they ask me why I left my other job?" she asked softly.

The very next day, I saw Isabel and reported to her on the meeting. "How did it feel going?" she asked.

"It was a relief to be with my own kind," I responded, "but to tell you the truth, the people I've met on the outside over the past year were just as nuts as them."

"So, you've found that other people have problems, too," said Isabel.

I could see where this was going, but I didn't mind.

"Yes, there are a lot of people who have it pretty bad," I said. "Much worse than me." And then I thought for a second of all the good things I had in my life—a half-deaf elderly neighbor who always held the elevator door open for me; a job that paid me a decent salary and allowed me to use some of my creativity; a family that supported me as best they could; and the potential to meet a loving man.

"And you are grateful for some things," said Isabel.

"Yes," I agreed. And then it occurred to me that it was all a matter of perception. It wasn't what happened to me that was the problem; it was strictly how I viewed these things and what importance I gave them. There was always an opportunity to feel gratitude if I reframed certain events. And feeling gratitude, I had learned, was the first real step toward happiness.

"Do you still want to go back to the hospital?" asked my therapist.

"No," I said. "I don't need such strict supervision. And anyway, there are much funnier stories on the outside."

"You've found something that makes you happy," said my therapist.

"What is it?" I said.

"You tell me."

"Well," I finally said, "this whole year has been kind of enjoyable in that I've been able to laugh at a whole bunch of people, myself included, making idiots of ourselves. And I've made some people laugh about that."

"So it brings you joy to make people laugh," said Isabel.

"Yes," I concurred. "And I'll still do that even if you move to California."

"You're not worried?" my therapist asked.

"I'm not worried," I said.

For a brief moment, Isabel's eyes danced. Maybe it was true that I had really grown over the past year. At least I had taken some gutsy risks that I hadn't thought possible, thereby cutting my Misery Gap in half. And while I wasn't yet in a state of "invulnerable euphoria"— there probably was no such thing—I was content. And that, I decided, was the best a person could ask for.

About the Author

Wendy Aron has been a professional writer for the past twenty years and has worked in virtually every medium, ranging from television sitcoms, to the stage, to journalism and advertising copywriting.

After college, she was selected for the highly competitive Screenwriting program at the UCLA Graduate School of Motion Pictures/TV. Upon leaving UCLA, Wendy wrote for the hit sitcom *Family Ties*, starring Michael J. Fox.

Mark Allen photo

In New York in the early nineties, she wrote for the theater, her comedic plays being produced at several off-off-Broadway Manhattan stages, including the American Theatre of Actors, the Sanford Meisner Theater, INTAR and the Theater-Studio.

More recently, Wendy has freelanced for *The New York Times* and *Newsweek* magazine and has worked as an advertising copywriter for Doubleday Direct. She is a member of the Authors Guild and the Dramatists Guild of America. Wendy lives in Oceanside, New York, with her husband and their three neurotic cats.

Bibliography

Aron, Elaine. *The Highly Sensitive Person* (Broadway, 1997).

A landmark work that shows you how to identify the highly sensitive trait in yourself and make the most of it in everyday situations.

Bourne, Edmund J. *The Anxiety & Phobia Workbook*, 4th ed. (New Harbinger, 2005).

An essential workbook that explains the cause and nature of anxiety disorders and offers self-help exercises and guidelines to overcome anxiety.

Brampton, Sally J. *Shoot the Damn Dog: A Memoir of Depression* (W.W. Norton, 2008).

A searing memoir that offers practical advice, hope and inspiration to those suffering from depression.

Burns, David D. *The Feeling Good Handbook* (Plume, 1999).

A powerful guide to techniques that can help you feel better about yourself and those you love, complete with step-by-step "feel good" exercises.

Burns, David D. *Ten Days to Self-Esteem* (Collins, 1999).

> An insightful presentation of innovative, clear and compassionate ways to help you identify the causes of your mood slumps and develop a more positive outlook on life.

....

Cronkite, Kathy. *On the Edge of Darkness: America's Most Celebrated Actors, Journalists and Politicians Chronicle Their Most Arduous Journey* (Delta, 1995).

> A moving series of true stories that prove you are not alone and that many famous people have also suffered from depression.

....

Leahy, Robert L. *The Worry Cure: Seven Steps to Stop Worry From Stopping You* (Harmony, 2005).

> A systematic and accessible guide to gaining control over debilitating anxiety.

....

Luciani, Joseph J. *Self-Coaching: How to Heal Anxiety and Depression* (Wiley, 2001).

> A great tool for tips on using positive self-talk and self-coaching to defeat anxiety and depression.

O'Connor, Richard. *Undoing Depression* (Berkley Trade, 1999).

A holistic approach to replacing depressive patterns of thinking, relating and behaving with a new and more effective set of skills.

....

Viscott, David. *Emotional Resilience: Simple Truths for Dealing with the Unfinished Business of Your Past* (Three Rivers Press, 1997).

A pragmatic handbook that shows you how to let go of past hurts and express your feelings in the moment.

Organizations

National Institute of Mental Health
Science Writing, Press, and Dissemination Branch
6001 Executive Boulevard, Room 8184, MSC 9663
Bethesda, MD 20892-9663
www.nimh.nih.gov/

> The largest scientific organization in the world dedicated to
> research focused on the understanding, treatment, and prevention
> of mental disorders and the promotion of mental health.

National Alliance on Mental Illness
Colonial Place Three
2107 Wilson Blvd. Suite 300
Arlington, Virginia 22201-3042
www.nami.org

> The nation's largest grassroots mental health organization
> dedicated to improving the lives of persons living with serious
> mental illness and their families. NAMI has over 1,000 local
> chapters nationwide.

Emotions Anonymous International
PO Box 4245
St. Paul, Minnesota 55104-0245
www.emotionsanonymous.org/

This is a nationwide twelve-step organization, similar to Alcoholics Anonymous. It is a fellowship composed of people who come together in weekly meetings for the purpose of working toward recovery from emotional difficulties.

The American Institute for Cognitive Therapy
136 East 57th St. Suite 1101
New York City, New York 10022
www.cognitivetherapynyc.com

An internationally recognized group of clinical psychologists and psychotherapists that provide cognitive-behavioral treatment for depression, anxiety, phobias, eating disorders, personality disorders, child and adolescent problems and family and marital problems.

Mental Health America
2000 N. Beauregard Street, 6th Floor
Alexandria, VA 22311
www.nmha.org/

The country's leading non-profit dedicated to helping all people live mentally healthier lives. It has over 320 affiliates nationwide.

The International Foundation for Research and Education on Depression (iFred)
2017-D Renard Ct.
Annapolis, MD 21401 USA
www.ifred.org/

A non-profit dedicated to researching causes of depression, supporting those dealing with the illness, and combating the stigma associated with it.

Depression and Bipolar Support Alliance (DBSA)
730 N. Franklin Street, Suite 501
Chicago, Illinois 60610-7224 USA
www.dbsalliance.org/

Patient-directed, it supports research on mental illness and gives scientifically based tools and information to help cope with it. DBSA also searches for cures and works to ensure that people living with mood disorders are treated equitably.

Anxiety Disorders Association of America
8730 Georgia Ave., Suite 600
Silver Spring, MD 20910
www.adaa.org/

A national non-profit dedicated to the prevention, treatment, and cure of anxiety disorders and to improving the lives of all people who suffer from them.

Web Sites

About.com Guide
http://depression.about.com/

Your best starting place for learning about symptoms and treatments for depression, as well as how to cope. Includes support forums, links, articles, newsletters and more.

Psychcentral.com
http://psychcentral.com/

The Internet's largest and oldest independent mental heath social networks created and run by mental health professionals.

Mental Help Net
www.mentalhelp.net

The Mental Help Net website exists to promote mental health and wellness education and advocacy.

Dr. Ivan's Depression Central
www.psycom.net/depression.central

A clearinghouse for information on all types of mood disorders and their most effective treatments, compiled by psychopharmacologist Ivan Goldberg.

....

Depression.com
www.depression.com

Facts about depression, including how to manage it and how to live with this medical condition.

....

Depression Health Center
www.webmd.com/depression

Here you'll find in-depth depression information including symptoms, medications, etc.

....

HelpGuide.org
www.helpguide.org/mental/anxiety_types_symptoms_ treatment.htm

Learn about the symptoms, causes, and types of anxiety attacks and disorders. Find self-help tips and anxiety treatment information.

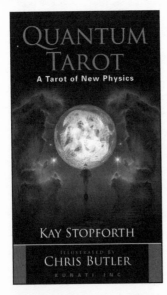

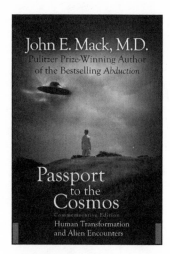

Passport to the Cosmos
Commemorative Edition: Human Transformation and Alien Encounters
■ John E. Mack M.D.

In this edition, with photos and new forewords, Pulitzer Prize–winner John E. Mack M.D. powerfully demonstrates how the alien abduction phenomenon calls for a revolutionary new way of examining the nature of reality and our place in the cosmos. "Fascinating foray into an exotic world. From Harvard psychiatry professor and Pulitzer Prize-winning author … based on accounts of abductions." —*Publishers Weekly*

US$ 14.95 | Pages 368 | Trade Paper 6x9"
ISBN 9781601641618

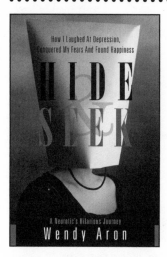

Hide & Seek
How I Laughed At Depression, Conquered My Fears and Found Happiness
■ Wendy Aron

Hide & Seek shows how to tackle important issues such as letting go of blame and resentment and battling negative thinking. Instructive without being preachy, it is filled with humor and pathos, and a healthy dose of eye-opening insight for the millions who suffer from depression and low self-esteem. "Learning how to cope with hopelessness has never been so fun." —*ForeWord*

US$ 14.95 | Pages 256 | Trade Paper 6x9"
ISBN 9781601641588

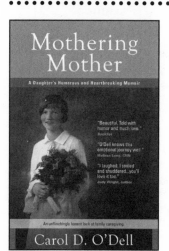

Mothering Mother
An unflinchingly honest look at family caregiving
■ Carol D. O'Dell

Mothering Mother is an authentic, "in-the-room" view of a daughter's struggle to care for a dying parent. It will touch you and never leave you.

"O'Dell portrays the experience of looking after a mother suffering from Alzheimer's and Parkinson's with brutal honesty and refreshing grace."—*Booklist*

US$ 12.95 | Pages 208 | Trade Paper 6x9"
ISBN 9781601640468

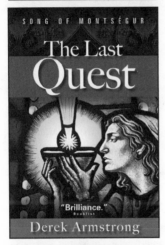

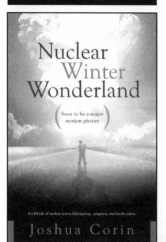

Nuclear Winter Wonderland
■ Joshua Corin

College senior Adam Weiss wants to be home for the holidays, when a lunatic nuclear terrorist kidnaps his twin sister Anna from a highway rest stop, Adam's plans take an abrupt twist. He soon meets up with two people willing to help him rescue his sister, a dyspeptic exmob thug and a Spanish-speaking female clown. Adam and his friends have just six days to save his sister—and the world—from a cancer-doomed maniac.
Soon to be a major motion picture.

US$ 15.95 | Pages 288 | Trade Paper 6x9"
ISBN 9781601641601

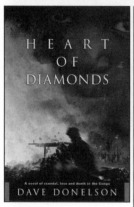

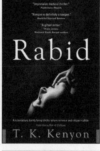

Rabid
■ T. K. Kenyon

"What begins as a riff on Peyton Place (salacious small-town intrigue) smoothly metamorphoses into a philosophical battle between science and religion. Kenyon is definitely a keeper." —*Booklist*
US$ 15.95 | Pages 480 | Trade Paper
ISBN 9781601640406

Bang Bang
■ Lynn Hoffman

"The literary equivalent of a Tarantino movie: edgy, streetwise, and a little arrogant, with a strong and determined female protagonist. Brilliant might be too big a word for this novel but not by much." —*Booklist*
US$ 12.95 | Pages 176 | Trade Paper
ISBN 9781601640284

Heart of Diamonds
■ Dave Donelson

Corruption at the highest levels of government, greed in the church and brutality among warring factions make the Congo a very dangerous place for television journalist Valerie Grey. *Heart of Diamonds* is a fast-paced tale of ambition, avarice, betrayal and love.

US$ 14.95
Pages 352 | Trade Paper 6x9"
ISBN 9781601641571

The Game
■ Derek Armstrong

"A mystery-thriller features a reality TV show, a murder and a cantakerous detective with a touch of House M.D. ... Armstrong compels us to keep reading ... keeps us chuckling. A series to watch." —*Booklist*
US$ 14.95 | Pages 352 | Trade Paper
ISBN 9781601640345

KÜNATI

MADicine
■ Derek Armstrong

What happens when an engineered virus, meant to virally lobotomize psychopathic patients, is let loose on the world? Only Bane and his new partner, Doctor Ada Kenner, can stop this virus of rage.

■ "Like Ian Fleming, he somehow combines over-the-top satire with genuinely suspenseful action … Celebrate the upcoming centenary of Ian Fleming's birth by reading this book." —STARRED REVIEW *Booklist*

■ "Tongue-in-cheek thriller." *The Game* —Library Journal

US$ 24.95 | Pages 352, cloth hardcover
ISBN 978-1-60164-017-8 | EAN: 9781601640178

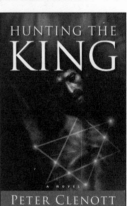

Bathtub Admirals
■ Jeff Huber

Are the armed forces of the world's only superpower really run by self-serving "Bathtub Admirals"? Based on a true story of military incompetence.

■ "Witty, wacky, wildly outrageous … A remarkably accomplished book, striking just the right balance between ridicule and insight." —Booklist

US$ 24.95
Pages 320, cloth hardcover
ISBN 978-1-60164-019-2
EAN 9781601640192

Belly of the Whale
■ Linda Merlino

Terrorized by a gunman, a woman with cancer vows to survive and regains her hope and the will to live.

■ "A riveting story, both powerful and poignant in its telling. Merlino's immense talent shines on every page." —Howard Roughan, Bestselling Author

US$ 19.95
Pages 208, cloth hardcover
ISBN 978-1-60164-018-5
EAN 9781601640185

Hunting the King
■ Peter Clenott

An intellectual thriller about the most coveted archeological find of all time: the tomb of Jesus.

■ "Fans of intellectual thrillers and historical fiction will find a worthy new voice in Clenott … Given such an auspicious start, the sequel can't come too soon." —ForeWord

US$ 24.95
Pages 384, cloth hardcover
ISBN 978-1-60164-148-9
EAN 9781601641489

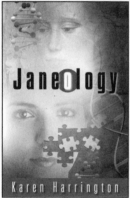

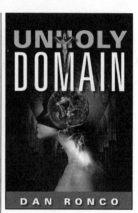

KÜNATI

Provocative. Bold. Controversial.

Kunati Book Titles

Available at your favorite bookseller

www.kunati.com

• •

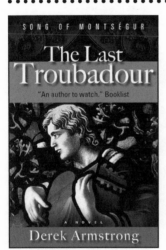

The Last Troubadour
Historical fiction by Derek Armstrong

Against the flames of a rising medieval Inquisition, a heretic, an atheist and a pagan are the last hope to save the holiest Christian relic from a sainted king and crusading pope. Based on true events.

■ "... brilliance in which Armstrong blends comedy, parody, and adventure in genuinely innovative ways." —*Booklist*

US$ 24.95 I Pages 384, cloth hardcover
ISBN-13: 978-1-60164-010-9
ISBN-10: 1-60164-010-2
EAN: 9781601640109

• •

Recycling Jimmy
A cheeky, outrageous novel by Andy Tilley

Two Manchester lads mine a local hospital ward for "clients" as they launch Quitters, their suicide-for-profit venture in this off-the-wall look at death and modern life.

■ "Energetic, imaginative, relentlessly and unabashedly vulgar." —*Booklist*
■ "Darkly comic story unwinds with plenty of surprises." —*ForeWord*

US$ 24.95 I Pages 256, cloth hardcover
ISBN-13: 978-1-60164-013-0
ISBN-10: 1-60164-013-7
EAN 9781601640130

Women Of Magdalene
A hauntingly tragic tale of the old South by Rosemary Poole-Carter

An idealistic young doctor in the post-Civil War South exposes the greed and cruelty at the heart of the Magdalene Ladies' Asylum in this elegant, richly detailed and moving story of love and sacrifice.

■ "A fine mix of thriller, historical fiction, and Southern Gothic." —*Booklist*
■ "A brilliant example of the best historical fiction can do." —*ForeWord*

US$ 24.95 I Pages 288, cloth hardcover
ISBN-13: 978-1-60164-014-7
ISBN-10: 1-60164-014-5 I EAN: 9781601640147

On Ice
A road story like no other, by Red Evans

The sudden death of a sad old fiddle player brings new happiness and hope to those who loved him in this charming, earthy, hilarious coming-of-age tale.

■ "Evans' humor is broad but infectious … Evans uses offbeat humor to both entertain and move his readers." —*Booklist*

US$ 19.95 I Pages 208, cloth hardcover
ISBN-13: 978-1-60164-015-4
ISBN-10: 1-60164-015-3
EAN: 9781601640154

Truth Or Bare
Offbeat, stylish crime novel by Richard Cahill

The characters throb with vitality, the prose sizzles in this darkly comic page-turner set in the sleazy world of murderous sex workers, the justice system, and the rich who will stop at nothing to get what they want.

■ "Cahill has introduced an enticing character … Let's hope this debut novel isn't the last we hear from him." —*Booklist*

US$ 24.95 I Pages 304, cloth hardcover
ISBN-13: 978-1-60164-016-1
ISBN-10: 1-60164-016-1
EAN: 9781601640161

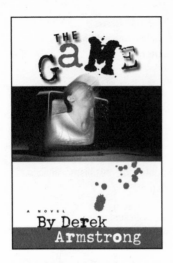

Provocative. Bold. Controversial.

The Game

A thriller by Derek Armstrong

Reality television becomes too real when a killer stalks the cast on America's number one live-broadcast reality show.
■ "A series to watch ... Armstrong injects the trope with new vigor." —*Booklist*
US$ 24.95 | Pages 352, cloth hardcover
ISBN 978-1-60164-001-7 | EAN: 9781601640017
LCCN 2006930183

● ●

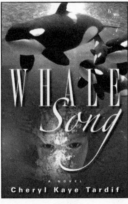

bang BANG	Whale Song	Shadow of
A novel by Lynn Hoffman	A novel by Cheryl Kaye Tardif	Innocence

bang BANG
A novel by Lynn Hoffman

In Lynn Hoffman's wickedly funny *bang-BANG*, a waitress crime victim takes on America's obsession with guns and transforms herself in the process. Read along as Paula becomes national hero and villain, enforcer and outlaw, lover and leader. Don't miss Paula Sherman's one-woman quest to change America.
■ "Brilliant"
—STARRED REVIEW, *Booklist*
US$ 19.95
Pages 176, cloth hardcover
ISBN 978-1-60164-000-0
EAN 9781601640000
LCCN 2006930182

Whale Song
A novel by Cheryl Kaye Tardif

Whale Song is a haunting tale of change and choice. Cheryl Kaye Tardif's beloved novel—a "wonderful novel that will make a wonderful movie" according to *Writer's Digest*—asks the difficult question, which is the higher morality, love or law?
■ "Crowd-pleasing ... a big hit."
—*Booklist*
US$ 12.95
Pages 208, UNA trade paper
ISBN 978-1-60164-007-9
EAN 9781601640079
LCCN 2006930188

Shadow of Innocence
A mystery by Ric Wasley

The Thin Man meets *Pulp Fiction* in a unique mystery set amid the drugs-and-music scene of the sixties that touches on all our societal taboos. *Shadow of Innocence* has it all: adventure, sleuthing, drugs, sex, music and a perverse shadowy secret that threatens to tear apart a posh New England town.
US$ 24.95
Pages 304, cloth hardcover
ISBN 978-1-60164-006-2
EAN 9781601640062
LCCN 2006930187